THE LONG AND
SHORT OF IT

Five Thousand Years of Fun and Fury over

☞ HAIR ☜

THE LONG AND

DAVID McKAY COMPANY, INC., NEW YORK

SHORT OF IT

*Five Thousand
Years of
Fun and Fury over*

HAIR

BY

Bill Severn

With over 100
illustrations

72 - 1343

OTHER BOOKS ON SOCIAL HISTORY BY

Bill Severn

PACKS OF FUN: 101 Unusual Things To Do
   With Playing Cards and To Know About Them

ROPE ROUNDUP: The Lore and Craft of Rope and Roping

MAGIC AND MAGICIANS

THE STORY OF THE HUMAN VOICE

HERE'S YOUR HAT

IF THE SHOE FITS

HAND IN GLOVE

Title page illustration: courtesy of Prints Division,
The New York Public Library, Astor, Lenox and Tilden Foundations

LIBRARY OF CONGRESS CATALOG CARD NO. 70-136007

MANUFACTURED IN THE UNITED STATES OF AMERICA

DESIGNED BY SOPHIE ADLER

Once Over Lightly

He wanted to be different from others, so he wore his hair long, but a band of men seized him and cut it off.

That might have happened yesterday. It also happened to the Biblical Samson.

Young people have "bad manners." Their hair is "atrocious."

Sound familiar? It was said in Greece more than two thousand years ago.

Women who wear wigs are out "to deceive the men" and should be made to stop such "a very wicked thing."

That complaint dates back to ancient Alexandria.

A young man appeared in court wearing a long beard and the judge ordered him from the courtroom to shave it off before he would hear the case.

It happened not long ago in the Midwest. It also happened in France in 1536.

The Massachusetts legislature has passed a law against long hair.

Tomorrow? No, the time was 1634.

Students at Harvard have been forbidden to wear long hair.

They were—in 1655.

Long-haired rebels are "savages" who should be barred from respectable homes.

Some Virginians thought that about the Minute Men of the Revolution.

The way young men and women wear their hair, it's hard to tell one sex from the other.

Many Americans were saying that in the 1950's, not because of long hair, but because both sexes cut it short.

Hair has been a cause of fury since history began. If one generation accepts long hair, the next insists it must be short; if young rebels wear beards, those who come next revolt against beards; if women sweep their hair high, younger women challenge conformity by combing it down. Always there have been some people who have tried to tell others how to wear their hair. Sometimes with rage, and sometimes with laughter, we have been getting into each other's hair for at least five thousand years.

Contents

The Beatles landed in New York in the spring of 1964, with the English haircuts that helped start the American long hair revolution. Considered startlingly long at the time, the Beatles' hair gradually grew much longer, as did the hair of millions of young Americans who were inspired to copy them. *United Press International, Inc.*

I

Four young Englishmen with modernized 15th century haircuts invaded the United States in the spring of 1964 as the shock troops of a hair revolution that divided America in battles for and against long hair that were fought through the rest of the decade.

Musicians John Lennon and Paul McCartney teamed up with Ringo Starr and George Harrison in Liverpool and in the early 1960s formed the Beatles. They reportedly took the advice of a girl friend of one of them to let their hair fall down over their foreheads. Soon their long-bobbed manes were swinging to a music which harnessed the hard rock beat to a fresh melodic and harmonic approach that had teen fans rioting with enthusiasm and chanting, "Yeah, yeah, yeah!"

They had their first million-record hit with "She Loves You" in 1963 and by the next April five of their records topped the charts in the United States. "Beatlemania," which spread over a good part of the world, came and went in America in five years, but by then the change in hair style had gone far beyond what the Beatles started.

When they invaded the United States in 1964 the Beatles were not teen-agers themselves; all four were men in their twenties. By 1970 they had outgrown their original hair-dos, and were going their separate ways in other endeavors. John Lennon's hair was tousled and short in a guru cut. Paul McCartney was comparatively short-haired and beard-less. George Harrison's hair was still long, but gathered neatly in a

1

pony tail. Ringo Starr, celebrating his thirtieth birthday in 1970, explained that he "just got bored" with long hair, so he had his wife cut it shorter than it had been in all his Beatle years. "It was driving me nuts," he said. "One day I found I just hated it."

The Beatles' 1964 invasion did not come without advance warning of what might happen to America's hair. They and other rock music groups already had gotten into Britain's hair. England had its teen-age Teddy boys, who dressed themselves in fancy Edwardian clothes and let their hair grow long at the backs of their necks while they piled the front of it up in curly mops. They were followed by the leather-jacketed, long-haired rockers, who roared around on motorcycles, when they weren't fighting teen gang wars with the smartly dressed scooter-riding mods, who considered their own hair and life style more "modish."

During the summer before the Beatles arrived in the United States half the teen population of London was wearing "Beatle crops, kitchen mops, shaggy locks, patchy thatches" and "hair as long as Lord Byron's." English school headmasters, shop foremen, military recruiting officers, and employment counselors complained. A police constable lopped off one boy's hair, some long-haired workers lost jobs, there was concern over "scruffiness," and a columnist said perhaps topless swimsuits had come just in time to identify one long-haired sex from the other.

American commentators, blind to what the Beatles were about to bring across the ocean, called long hair "a British phenomenon." *Look* magazine suggested that it might be a protest of male virility against "the sun setting over the British Empire." In the United States, hair was still generally short, when not crew cut. Some American college men had adopted the Caesar cut, with hair brushed in every direction from the center of the crown, much the way ancient Romans once had worn it. But there was little public awareness of what was soon to come. America's only really popular longhair was Prince Valiant, and he was still a character in the comic strips.

Within months after the landing of the Beatles, male moptops began a sprout-out and by the spring of 1965 the American crew cut was dying if not dead. What had started with the youngest teen followers of rock groups quickly spread to the whole young generation. A Chicago barber found eighty per cent of his young customers asking for long cuts and another barber in Massachusetts who specialized in shearing Harvard men said, "There's no place to use a clipper. There's no scalp to get close to." According to an oarsman at an Eastern college, "Not even members of crews have crew cuts."

There were greasers who drenched their hair with oil and lotions, surfers who never sullied their waving locks with a drop, and those who carried combs, pocket mirrors and cans of hair spray wherever they went. With some male teens spending as much time and money on their hair as girls, the once ruggedly masculine barbershop began to put hair-netted boys under dryers to set teased and sculpted hair-dos formed with razors instead of scissors and clippers.

Protests had already begun. Parents were viewing with alarm. School principals were delivering stern assembly hall lectures. And the elder intellectuals once disdainfully called "longhairs" found themselves outnumbered by youth. Soon there were the hippies and beatniks, most of whom let their hair grow into birds' nests and Biblical waves without artificial styling. The short-haired older generation tended to lump all young longhairs together and call them "revolting." And a revolt it was. Hair had become both a Declaration of Independence from the ways of the past and a symbolic Bill of Rights for individual freedoms.

Girls joined the revolution, first with male-matching Beatle bobs, then with hair that went straight. Those who had always been envied for their naturally curly locks suddenly discovered they were outcasts of teen fashion. Tresses that had been teased, tortured, and spray-cemented into bouffants came tumbling down in lank hanks.

In place of the curling irons that traditionally had helped a girl to keep a curl right in the middle of her forehead, clothes-pressing irons came into use to keep out the curl. High-schoolers and college girls were laying their locks across home ironing boards to have friends iron their hair as flat as a bedsheet. Done a few inches at a time, the process took half an hour, left hair very straight, fine and soft, and usually lasted until the next washing. At colleges girls lined up in dorms, waiting their turn to bend head to ironing board. "Even girls with straight hair," said one in a Connecticut school, "are ironing it to make it straighter."

Hairdressers offered beauty shop anti-permanents for twenty-five dollars a treatment and cosmetic manufacturers rushed home hair-straighteners to market at two dollars a jar. High fashion at first held aloof while some of its stylists searched back through history for eccentric hair-dos that continued to pile both real and false hair atop feminine heads. But lank-haired models, appearing in women's magazines, encouraged other women to follow the teen lead toward straight hair.

Blacks had been straightening their hair for years, dominated by styles set by a white society. But as whites rushed to straighten their hair, many blacks let theirs grow out naturally, in a demand for new freedoms and to identify with their own cultural past. The Afro, inspired by an-

3

A 1970 Afro style, a place winner among championship American haircuts, created by St. Louis, Mo., stylist Stanley Luckeh (Local 102). *Barbers, Beauticians and Allied Industries International Ass'n., AFL-CIO-CLC*

cestral styles native for centuries to peoples of East Africa, developed attractive variations for men and women, reflecting pride in being black as well as beauty.

Barbers gloomily predicted long hair would doom the barbershop. Some young men went without haircuts, trimmed each other's hair or had it done by girl friends, and those who did still visit the barber stretched the time between cuttings. By one estimate, shops across America were being forced to close at the rate of one hundred a month. While barbers' unions conducted publicity campaigns to emphasize the rewards of good grooming, many old-fashioned haircutters who failed to keep up with changing times faced empty chairs and bankruptcy.

But others who modernized their methods and surroundings found business and income booming. Instead of the traditional quick trim, they offered consultation in the styling and care of the new long coiffure and turned their establishments into masculine beauty shops. Young men with money to spend, and older men who began to let their hair lengthen in the wishful pursuit of youth, discovered what women always had known, that long hair required attention.

To convince a man that his errand was not just to get a haircut but to be part of a whole new "in" scene, many establishments became salons of lush luxury. Some provided such varied enticements as indoor putting greens, dart boards, chess tables, archery targets, art displays, model car racing, horoscope charts, free snacks and drinks, television viewing lounges, piped-in music, pretty hostesses, and tickers that tapped out news bulletins, sports results, and stock market reports.

Services included individual styling, hair problem and hair personality analysis, waving, straightening, thinning, restoring, conditioning, coloring, massage, sunlamp tanning, facials, and mudpacks. For patrons to buy and take home there were masculine perfumes, lotions, astringents, skin creams, tubes of liquid makeup in sun bronze and wind buff, and face powders to improve sallow or too-ruddy complexions.

For middle-aged men the sideburn often was the first step toward more hairiness, and some stopped with that, hoping to show by the whiskers in front of their ears that they were attuned to youth while clinging to the respectability of moderate haircuts. "Sideburns are

4

A far cry from the old-fashioned barbershop was this olive green and gold reception lounge of Earl's International in St. Louis, with its pecan wood furniture, busts of David and Hermes, antiques, and original water-color paintings. Some of its famous patrons regularly flew private planes half-way across the country to have their hair cared for by Earl Roach, named men's hairstylist of the year in 1970. *Earl E. Roach*

creeping across America like crabgrass," *Life* commented editorially in 1968, "wispy strands inching past the ear and down the cheek of men and teen-age boys, each one a pennant proclaiming, however seedily, that inside the impersonal shell there lives a person." Beards and moustaches, rare for half a century, also grew again, "unruly tangles, unsure of their destination," but proliferating so that "you can see a hundred beards coming down Fifth Avenue in any five minute span."

Millions of heads had hair that wasn't their own, wigs of synthetic fibers that looked and felt like hair but could be washed and hung to dry like laundry. Young career girls were the first big customers for the new inexpensive pull-ons, sold in hundreds of stores that never sold wigs

5

before. Most women chose them in colors to match their own hair but in styles to suit changing moods, and most men seemed to approve, although some husbands complained of not being sure whether the wife they came home to in the evening would be a blonde, a brunette, or a redhead.

Some men who saw girls wearing them wanted wigs themselves, which brought a moderate demand for women's wigs trimmed short and styled to fit men. Then a Manhattan department store, in the spring of 1970, ran small advertisements announcing stretch wigs made especially for men, and drew such eager lines of males to its doors that more than a thousand were sold in a week. Fittings, with stylists snipping here and there, took fifteen minutes. As the boom spread across the country there were predictions that men soon would be buying wigs as casually as neckties.

Many men wore wigs for the same reasons girls did, for the quick convenience of an ever-ready attractive appearance, or to change styles to suit mood or moment. Some, forced by day to cut their hair to moderate length for business, wanted long-haired wigs to wear nights and weekends, the better to impress girls, or just to be "with it." Others, with need for a temporary short-haired look, reversed the process and pinned their naturally long hair up under short wigs. Hundreds of pull-on wigs were sold to bald men who took to the new cover-ups to look younger.

For America's twenty million balding males, many of whom were suddenly self-conscious in an age of long-haired youth, there were also more expensive individual toupees, securely held in place with double-faced tape or with loops of surgical suture stitched to the scalp so that they could be "worn with confidence while swimming or in bed." Another disguise for baldness was hair weaving, which crocheted false hair into what was left of a man's own hair to cover his bald spot. And for those willing to pay the surgical fee and to undergo a series of sometimes painful operations over several months, there were hair transplants. Twenty roots at a time, plugs of hair were removed from the sides or back of a man's head, to be planted surgically where he was bald, with the hope that new hair would grow where none had been.

Americans fought over long hair in classrooms, courtrooms, places of employment, and in nearly every home with a son or daughter. The

Those who didn't grow them naturally soon wore false ones. The sideburned stretch wig, as well as the moustache and goatee, are imitations, styled by Jerry Piatt of San Diego, California's Razor's Edge Salon (Local 256). *Barbers, Beauticians and Allied Industries International Ass'n., AFL-CIO-CLC*

Army, Navy, Air Force and Marines went to war against it. Hair became a force in political campaigns, in advertising, on stage and screen. Poll-takers, psychologists, sociologists, columnists, and commentators spilled out millions of words about it. Few conflicts in American life got so much continuing attention as the emotional feuding over how the young should wear their hair.

School officials from California to Texas and from Maine to Florida generally took a determined stand for the old-fashioned short haircut. Some segregated long-haired students in the "solitary confinement" of unused study halls to keep them from attending classes they were accused of "distracting." Others suspended or expelled them, kept seniors from commencement exercises unless they cut their hair, refused them diplomas.

Demanding the right to wear their hair as they pleased, one hundred and fifty students of a Michigan high school walked out on strike. At a Wisconsin school, doors were barred to those with long hair. A Connecticut principal marched through his school, pulled more than fifty long-haired boys out of their classrooms, and ordered them not to come back until their hair was short. At a New Hampshire school, eighteen were forced to board a bus for a mass trip to the barber. In other places, a few principals or teachers personally sheared the hair from boys' heads.

Entire communities were divided, with enraged parents taking sides. In some schools, exact lengths and styles were specified: hair in front must have a width of one finger over the eyebrows, no hair overlapping the collar in back, sideburns at mid-ear level. Laws, which were different in every state, often limited how far schools could go in governing "conduct and behavior."

To many of the older generation, the question was not length of hair but proper respect for authority, maintaining standards, decorum, discipline, and classroom control. As a Norwalk, Connecticut, school system director put it in 1968, "The setting of values and guidelines for the community's youth is part of the educational process . . . a basic responsibility of the public schools."

On the other side were parents and educators who considered anti-hair edicts an attempt by government to dictate personal lives, to usurp family decisions, invade individual privacy, enforce conformity, and crush youthful questioning or dissent. By trying to tell students how to wear their hair, some charged, schools created problems of discipline and caused rebellion. Others saw more serious dangers, government violation of civil liberties and of basic constitutional rights, and the

7

threat that a school which tried to make all students wear hair alike was only a step away from telling them to think alike.

"Education is too important to be granted on the basis of personal appearance," the American Civil Liberties Union declared. "Dress and personal adornment are forms of self-expression: the freedom of personal preference should be guaranteed along with other liberties." The right of schools to maintain discipline gave school officials no legal basis for imposing standards of taste about hair style, the ACLU contended, and the situation was serious "when government tries to assert power that it does not possess."

Court cases, in many of which the ACLU offered advice and counsel, left the issue at least temporarily unresolved. State and municipal courts varied in their rulings, some questioning school authority and others upholding anti-hair regulations. The United States Supreme Court refused to review several decisions by Federal courts, some for and some against, but among those it left standing was a Court of Appeals ruling that students in a Wisconsin high school could not be expelled because they failed to get haircuts. "The right to wear one's hair at any length or in any desired manner," said the decision, "is an ingredient of personal freedom protected by the United States Constitution."

While courtroom battles continued and some schools went on fighting the hair war in the classrooms, other schools gradually eased their regulations. By sheer weight of numbers, if nothing else, the longhairs appeared to be winning. With male teachers, college professors, and middle-aged bankers and businessmen wearing their hair long, school skirmishes subsided. There were still flare-ups, especially in rural areas, but by 1970 in most city high school corridors and on college campuses there was hardly a short-hair in sight. "Hair," said one school official, "is over the hill. Even the fathers who come to PTA meetings have long hair."

Ever since the First World War, young Americans who entered the armed services had grumbled over having their hair clipped short, and the long-haired revolution changed the grumble to a roar. The military insisted on close-cropped uniformity for reasons of discipline, personal cleanliness, and the possible need to don helmets or other combat headgear. Resisters complained of being denied their human individuality by too-strict regulations. Some said that in off-duty hours they found themselves shunned by other young people, especially by girls, because of military haircuts. Many felt they had been made social outcasts among long-haired friends, particularly as opposition grew against the war in Vietnam.

8

Military haircuts allowed more freedom of style after the Army redefined its standards in the spring of 1970. Faces were to be clean shaven except for a moustache not longer than the one shown in the picture at the left. The center picture shows maximum length permitted for hair atop the head. At the right is the allowed sideburn, to be "neatly trimmed with straight lines and no flare at the base." *Army News Features*

Examples were made of men who disobeyed haircut orders. In some cases, they were court-martialed, fined, sentenced to imprisonment at hard labor. In the reserve forces, men protested against having to cut their hair short for a few days of military service a month, which left them short-haired all the rest of the time as civilians. The threat hung over them that if they failed to appear for reserve drills with short hair they might lose their reserve standing and be drafted into regular services, possibly be sent to risk their lives in war for lack of a haircut.

With the hope of getting around the regulations, some reservists bought short-haired wigs, so they could tuck their long hair under them during days when they had to pass inspection by drill sergeants. Wig shops near military bases also reported a brisk sale of long-haired wigs to full-time soldiers, midshipmen, and marines for wearing while on leave. Some reserve officers took a tolerant attitude and ignored wigs as long as men on duty appeared to meet required standards.

In the spring of 1970 the Army redefined its hair regulations, to allow somewhat more freedom of choice in the style of haircuts. Half a dozen specified styles were permitted, with a maximum hair length of three inches, and there was a slight retreat on moustaches and the dimensions of sideburns. But the announcement made it clear that the new regulations would be strictly enforced and that there was to be no total long-haired freedom for locks to sprout in defiance of neat and orderly appearance.

Three-inch lengths also were the rule in the Navy, Air Force, and Marines, but with some differences among the services about permitted growths of facial hair. In the Navy, restrained beards were accepted. Marines were allowed a "noneccentric moustache," but no beards or "long or conspicuous sideburns."

Resistance to long-haired youth produced roadside billboards in 1968, picturing an exceptionally shaggy-haired hippie, with an admonition for

9

him to get a haircut as part of the "beautification" of America. Some billboards were locally sponsored, others donated as a "public service" by an outdoor advertising company.

Newspapers tended to play the hair controversy for laughs, with stories about fathers buying dog licenses for long-haired sons, mothers presenting boys with pink hairnets in attempts to shame them, parents failing to recognize their own hairy offspring who came home on vacations from college, school officials mistaking long-haired boys for girls and reprimanding them for using the wrong washrooms, and wise-cracking magistrates who accused longhairs of "disturbing the peace."

A big West Coast amusement park stationed security guards at its gates to turn away hundreds of young people because their long hair "stood out in a crowd, caused comment, led to problems with other guests," although the same park used long-haired musicians to attract customers to the box office. In towns where anniversary celebrations were held some businessmen refused to join in traditional beard-growing contests for fear public disapproval might link them with long-haired youth. Some public swimming pools barred long-haired bathers or forced young men to put on girls' bathing caps before entering the water.

More serious were isolated cases where sheriffs or police took it upon themselves to shave and barber teen-aged heads. Private rage against long hair in some sections of the country also turned men to beating

Some citizens considered it a public service to urge young Americans to cut their hair, and billboarded their pleas with roadside signs such as this one which appeared near the railroad station in Norwalk, Connecticut, in 1968. *United Press International, Inc.*

10

or scalping hitch-hikers. Long-haired motorists stopping in small towns often found themselves threatened. Bullying men roamed beaches and picnic areas hunting down longhairs to menace.

Among the determined foes of long hair were discipline-minded high school gym teachers and college athletic coaches. Across the country they were almost unanimous in demanding haircuts and clean-shaven faces "for team morale and unity." A California college football coach said he would order players with long hair to take the field without protective helmets. Another in Oregon touched off a revolt in which athletes threatened to quit the campus after a player was ordered to shave beard and moustache.

In Maryland, the star of a basketball team was benched because of his hair style. A record-breaking sprinter with long hair was dropped from a West Coast team. Two runners who refused to shave moustaches were ousted from the track squad of an Illinois university. Official entry rules for a Pacific tennis tournament in 1969 were: "All boys are required to be clean-shaven and to have short haircuts."

But as in other school battles over hair, many coaches found they gradually had to adjust to change. School athletes in the 1970s were refusing to accept rules against hair choice that were contrary to what had become the hair styles of a young majority. Evidence of change was the national collegiate track and field championship won in June, 1970, by a University of California team of goateed and moustached sprinters, sideburned and long-haired runners and jumpers.

When it came to getting a job or keeping one, the price often was a haircut. A major airline threatened to discharge stewardesses whose hair style conflicted with grooming regulations, and did fire one who refused to change her Afro. In New England, an insurance company informed sales representatives that moderate hair length was a condition of employment. Telephone installers in New York were told they must keep hair short to avoid customer complaints. The head of an agency hiring college boys for high-paying summer jobs in Catskill mountain resort hotels warned that shoulder-length hair and moustaches were not wanted, and asked job-seekers, "What is more important, your hair or the possibility of making good money to pay for your education?"

Police departments in several cities cracked down on individualists who chose to wear long hair, as did some municipal transit systems, but after arbitration of their complaints New York bus drivers were permitted to choose their own hair styles and to wear beards, sideburns and other "facial foliage," as long as they were neatly trimmed.

In the San Francisco area a clerk for a chain supermarket rallied

11

customers to his support and won a long battle against bosses who wanted him to cut off his long hair. But in another California area a state unemployment insurance office ruled that jobless men with long hair could no longer collect unemployment benefits, after a survey of nine hundred employers showed most of them would refuse to hire anyone whose hair was not neatly trimmed at neck and ear.

Popular songs already had made the fight to wear long hair a symbol of youth's protest when the theatrical production *Hair,* billed as a "love-rock musical," burst upon the New York stage in April, 1968, to make its statement of the new life. Its fresh music, words, and a hint of nudity, delivered a shock message across the footlights to delight the young and bewilder some of the not-so-young. More than two years later *Hair*'s audiences were still crowding the theater to standing room only while other companies carried its new generation image around the world.

On the screen, hair become a movie theme. *Alice's Restaurant* had its star thrown through a plate glass window by young toughs who objected to his long hair. *Easy Rider* pictured two young motorcyclists who, because of long hair, were harassed and eventually killed. Playing it more for comedy, Dick Van Dyke in *Some Kind of A Nut* portrayed a bank teller bucking the conservative establishment by wearing a beard. Among those who got the message and made the most of hair commercially were the advertising agencies. Hair on the heads of young models in magazine advertisements and television commercials soon grew considerably longer.

Politically hair could be dangerous. Some national leaders wore hair moderately long, tousled over the forehead, Kennedy style, and an outstanding exception among generally short-haired older politicians was white-maned veteran Senator Everett Dirksen. But prejudice against long hair was so strong among the nation's voting majority that some of the young crusaders who campaigned in the 1968 primary election battles for Eugene McCarthy and against war in Vietnam sacrificed their hair to help spread the word. They went "clean for Gene" with haircuts, lest their hair get in the way of reasoned discourse with adult voters whose doorbells they rang.

The 1970 congressional battles brought complaints to the Fair Campaign Practices Committee that some candidates were using television commercials to picture their opponents surrounded by longhairs who had nothing to do with their campaigns. Long hair, it was charged, had become a tactic of "guilt-by-association." There were complaints of attempts "to pose a phony picture of a candidate with long-haired students" and reports that opponents were distributing "a candidate's

12

A ceremonial shearing of long hair as portrayed by members of the cast of the musical *Hair,* which had its 1000th New York performance in September, 1970, and by then had been seen by more than ten million people around the world.   *From the musical "Hair"*

picture with long-haired students, identifying them as helpers, when in fact they were merely members of the audience."

American long hair meanwhile had become an international "infection" that aroused government authority around the world. Borders were guarded to prevent vacationing young Americans from carrying long hair across them. Cities and nations battled long hair as if it were a spreading disease that if left unchecked might destroy their young. Traveling Americans often found foreign officials more strict about hair than those at home, particularly in countries where authoritarian regimes treated any kind of non-conformity as a crime.

Even friendly Mexico, long dependent upon American tourist trade, stopped hippie-type longhairs at its borders. Official government policy denied tourist cards to such "undesirables." Border guards informed offending longhairs they could not enter unless they got haircuts and shaves. Some guards taunted long-haired boys by calling them *señoritas*. In the Mexican town of San Miguel de Allende, where an art school attracted a large number of visiting Americans, the mayor took it upon himself in 1969 to have police seize all long-haired males, take them to headquarters, and shave them.

Brazilian police in Rio de Janeiro also picked up mopheads on the streets and took them in for haircuts. Men in Argentina wearing hair regarded as unduly long were regularly arrested, booked, and given haircuts. In Chile there were crackdowns in resort areas where officials acted to keep young Chileans from imitating American hair styles. Elsewhere in Latin America conservative short-haired visitors from the United States found it easier to get around than those with long hair.

In Europe, Communist-dominated countries were the most severe, with longhairs halted at the borders of both Czechoslovakia and Bulgaria. Sideburns were accepted in Bulgaria, but not excess hair at the nape of the neck. In Russia itself, the propaganda mills denounced as enemies of the state "rogues, spongers, and bearded ex-students."

Liberal France did not ban arriving longhairs, but customs officials and police closely questioned them with Gallic chill after the French student upheavals of 1968. Greece frowned upon long-haired visitors and discouraged long hair among its own people. Austria, except for Vienna, made young Americans with long hair unwelcome, with citizens of Alpine regions sometimes banding together to run them out. Nine out of ten Austrians, according to a 1970 public opinion poll, favored barring foreign "hippies" from entering the country.

14

Italy, after a campaign by conservatives against the long-haired *zazzerone,* grew more tolerant as Italian youth became increasingly long-haired. There was also tolerance in England, where it all began, and tolerance if not encouragement in Amsterdam, a summer mecca for thousands of longhairs from America and all over Europe. Scandinavia seemed to regard them as amusing rather than threatening.

War against long hair raged across most of Asia from mainland China to South Vietnam. In Red China, to promote the philosophy that looking alike encourages thinking alike and acting alike, Red Guards administered "pro-Peking" haircuts. Elsewhere it was the "pollution" of Asian youth by the American longhairs they were copying that officials gave as the reason for forcibly cutting the hair of their own teen-agers and barring entrance to young Americans they considered a bad influence.

Long-haired youths in Hong Kong were subject to arrest on the streets, and Indonesia and Thailand also dealt with them sternly. In Taiwan, where a motion picture was held from release because an actor's hair was too long, both beards and hair came under police regulation, with offenders first warned and then jailed or deported if they failed to visit a barber. To "combat juvenile delinquency," Portuguese Macao adopted a "big shears" policy of cutting the hair of any youth who got into trouble with the law for any reason.

The Island Republic of Singapore, proclaiming itself a "bastion of resistance to the social pollution of hippies," had police arrest longhairs and give them jail haircuts, officially refused entry to all long-haired foreigners, banned long-haired entertainers from television, encouraged shops and government clerks to cold-shoulder anyone with long hair, and suggested that young people "take a good look at themselves in the mirror." But when three youths from neighboring Malaysia were caught in the roundup, jailed and barbered, there was such an uproar the Malaysian government filed a formal protest, and Singapore's prime minister was forced to cancel an important diplomatic visit to Malaysia.

Saigon police, some of whom used bayonets to shear heads on the spot, arrested and forced haircuts upon more than fourteen hundred South Vietnamese youths within three weeks in the fall of 1970. The mass roundups "to eradicate social vices" put "young men having hippie hairdos" on the same daily list of offenders as gamblers, prostitutes, opium smokers, and beggars. To "preserve Vietnamese culture and social customs," the South Vietnamese government also decreed that long-haired foreign males were to be banned from the country as "a bad example for

our boys," and instructed all airlines to advise anybody bound for Saigon to get a haircut or stay away.

"It's a passing fad, just a wave," said one hair stylist, but the wave rolled on, long after the first coming of the Beatles. "Hair is the traditional symbol of male strength," another said, "and a blessing for boys who otherwise would look bleak and ordinary."

To some, long hair was youth's chip on the shoulder, a new generation's traditional challenge of the old. Others saw it as an outward sign of deeper revolt against everything wrong with the world as it was, a rebellion against parents and older people blamed by youth for the ills of society, against the short-cropped military, the conforming short-haired establishment. But there were those who argued that long hair in itself was a conformity, motivated by youth's insecurity and teen social pressures that demanded being part of a group.

"They want to cling to childhood as long as they can to avoid the terrifying responsibilities of having to make individual adult decisions in an atomic age," a psychologist suggested. Among other attempts to explain long hair in psychological terms was that it represented the preservation of the male life-urge, was a symbolic defense against a world that threatened death, or that there was an escape from smothering mother love in a boy's refusal to get a haircut "to please mom," or a wish to blur the lines distinguishing the two sexes, or an urge to seek a softer, gentler, less materialistic life.

Some sociologists found in long hair a healthy rejection of the stylized images of television and slick magazines that too often prettified people and problems and brought youth's disgust with the "phony façade of a plastic and pre-packaged make-believe world which has little to do with truth and reality." It was parents who were accused by others of making too much of external appearances, of trying to force young people to conform to styles that satisfied a wish to live through their children, of expressing their fears in a bewildering fast-changing world by making long hair the scapegoat of their mass rejection of change.

Biologists wondered if man were coming into his "biological destiny" of the male in nature, the bird "who spreads his gorgeous tail feathers" to captivate his inconspicuous mate. But a counter theory was that girls wanted boys to wear hair as long as their own "to establish an equality that eliminates the dominant cave-man male as ruler of all females he surveys."

From the musical "Hair"

17

Less analytical was a boy who said, "My hair is mine. I have a right to wear it as I please. I wear it long because I like it that way, that's all." And a mother in Tennessee, questioned by a national pollster who rang her doorbell, dismissed him with the comment, "Hair, schmair, why the fuss? In twenty years the kids will all be bald."

Obviously there could be no one explanation. Young people wore hair long for as many different reasons as there were styles of it. To some, it was a protest, but others were protesting nothing. Underlying the whole controversy was the historic fact that hair forever had been a battleground of mankind. It provided one of the oldest continuing conflicts of human existence.

The parting of a man's hair had been a real generation gap since time began. Whether he wore it long or short, went bearded or not, and what women did with their hair, caused a never-ending fury. In almost every age, people were seized, stoned, jailed, denounced, dragged into court, forced out of jobs, punished by schools and military services, and shunned by the establishment for daring to wear their hair in ways that were different from others.

☞ II ☜

It began with Adam, who according to early tradition was created long-haired and bushy-bearded. The Biblical tale of man's beginning in the Garden of Eden says nothing about Adam's hair, but since hair and beard were symbols of manliness to the ancients they took it for granted that he was created with a good growth of hair and that his rib, Eve, also was given flowing tresses. The arguments came later, and went on for centuries, as philosophers, artists, and theologians seriously debated the state of Adam's hair at the time of creation.

The hair controversy was in full rage by early Biblical days. Everybody knows what happened to the mighty Samson. Like other devout Nazarites, he had taken an oath to let his hair grow long. He told his woman, Delilah, that from the time he was born he had never had a haircut because he didn't want to be "like any *other* man."

"If I be shaven," he protested, "then my strength will go from me." But Delilah accepted a bribe from the lords of the Philistines, lulled Samson to sleep, and called for a barber to shave off his seven locks of hair. It "began to grow again after it was shaven," but by then it was too late. With his hair cut, Samson was just like any Philistine.

David, the giant-killer who became King of Israel, waged a terrible war because a bold heathen shaved some of his men. He had sent ambassadors on a mission to King Hanun of the Ammonites. But Hanun was suspicious of the bearded delegation. Convinced that they were spies,

Delilah, triumphant, after cutting off Samson's hair.

he ordered one-half of each man's beard shaved off before he let them go. When David learned what had happened, he sent his men a message to save face and hide their shame: "Tarry ye at Jericho until your beards are grown." In the war that followed, David's forces destroyed eight thousand enemy chariots, killed forty thousand men, and seized the Ammonite capital.

King David's rebellious son Absalom got a haircut only once a year, on his birthday, and in a year's time the hair he grew weighed two hundred shekels, almost four pounds. Absalom plotted to overthrow his father and make himself king, but his long hair caught him up. He rode a mule into battle against his father's troops, got his wild hair tangled in the branch of an oak tree, and while he was hanging there was speared to death.

20

Hanun deals with David's messengers.

Absalom caught by his hair in the tree.

21

King David's lament became a classic expression of paternal grief: "Oh my son Absalom, my son, . . . would God I had died for thee. . . ." It inspired paintings, plays, novels, and poetry. It also inspired English wigmakers of the 18th century to suggest Absalom would have been much better off wearing a wig. An irreverent satire posted in barbershops of that later time went:

> Oh, Absalom! Oh, Absalom!
> Oh, Absalom! My son,
> If thou hadst worn a periwig,
> Thou hadst not been undone!

The earliest Egyptians wore their hair as it grew, long and wavy, and paid little attention to it, except that men sometimes stuck an ostrich plume in it for decoration. This was one way to tell men from women in a land where everybody wore skirts.

But gradually hair styles became more and more elaborate, until finally some daring individual decided it was all too much bother and put on a wig. Pretty soon nearly all Egyptian men and women were shaving their heads and donning wigs, which were a lot more comfortable than long natural hair in a hot climate. The wigs were well air-conditioned as they were made on network caps to provide ventilation.

Baldness, instead of being a blight, became the accepted custom, and Egyptians came to hate hair so much they made shaving it off part of their religion. Those who failed to keep their heads shaved offended not only their elders but also the gods. Egyptian priests had their heads and entire bodies shaved at least three times a week. Young boys, required to wear a long lock of natural hair hanging to the right shoulder, could hardly wait to have the barber remove it so they could join the bald ranks of manhood.

A shave and a haircut were all one thing to the Egyptians whose dislike of hair and desire to be bald made them constant customers of the barber. Wealthy men and women were visited daily by barbers

Egyptian barbers, shaving the head, and applying perfumed wax to help cool it and hold a wig in place.

22

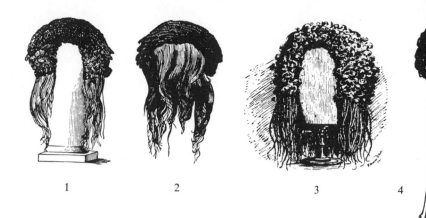

Egyptian wigs. The caplike upper parts were of tightly curled hair or wool, and the sides looser. Numbers 1 and 2 front and back views of the same wig. Number 3 probably was a woman's wig. Number 4 shows a long wig.

who shaved or plucked the hair from their heads. For those who couldn't afford house calls, there were open air barbershops where patrons about to be shorn sat beneath sheltering palm trees. Hair was not only shunned but was considered evil.

Wigs were meant to look false, not to imitate natural hair but to show Egyptian contempt for all that was hairy. Black was the usual color, but some were dyed red, green, or blue. Natural long hair was so abhorred that Egyptians let their own hair grow out only in times of mourning the dead, to show their grief and set themselves apart from others. But they literally refused to be caught dead with their heads unwigged, and were buried with wigs on, suitably attired to meet the gods of the hereafter.

Over the years the braiding and curling of Egyptian wigs became highly stylized. Rigid codes of appearance denoted the rank, position and social standing of a person according to the way he wore his false hair. Then as now, society raged against those who dared to be different about hair, even though all hair was fake. Some nobles, including several queens, went wigless and bald. But for the majority of conventional Egyp-

LEFT This wig-do was the Lotus style, popular with Egyptian women. RIGHT An even more elaborate covering head-dress, the Peacock.

23

tians, wigs were no escape from the restrictions that in earlier centuries had governed hair styles. They became as elaborate as the shorn-off locks they had replaced.

Egyptian beards, which had flourished in earlier times, also went the way of the razor, with stylized false beards to take their place. Since early kings had worn beards, later kings wore false beards. Some Egyptian queens, perhaps insisting on equality of the sexes, also wore them.

Fake beards

Natural beards were hated as much as natural hair. Wall paintings traditionally pictured the nation's enemies as hairy men, to be conquered and trampled upon by bald and clean-faced Egyptians. The wandering Greek historian, Herodotus, noted that Egyptians were horrified by the hairy Greeks of his time. Beards made Greek faces so repulsive to the Egyptians, he wrote, that not an Egyptian man or woman would kiss a Greek.

Ancient Greek men wore hair so long they had to braid it in topknots on the crowns of their heads and hold it in place with hairpins. The brave Spartans spent hours combing out their long hair before they went into battle. Achilles, although weak in the heel, had such beautiful long hair it was likened to his bravery in the Trojan Wars. Strong man Hercules was pictured as having the hair of a bull, and Homer called the Greeks "the long-haired ones."

With that tradition, it seemed nothing less than a denial of the hairy virility of the heroic past when young men began to shave their beards and cut their hair short. The learned old men were outraged by what seemed to them a sign of effeminate weakness that was undermining the strength of the nation.

When Diogenes went walking the streets of Corinth, shining a lantern into faces in his search for an honest man, he also searched for those who wore their hair and beards long, as he believed any he-man should. He had plenty of hair on his own head and face and he let those without it know exactly what he thought of them. When Diogenes spotted a Greek youth with the new clean-cut look that disgusted him, his favorite question was: "Have you shaved because you are disappointed you were created a man instead of a woman?"

Shaving had been hardly known in Greece until Alexander the Great commanded his soldiers to shave in the 4th century B.C. He had good military reasons. In the close hand-to-hand fighting of those days long beards were up for grabs, so Alexander ordered his troops "to remove the handle which the enemy can seize." Civilians quickly imitated the military look and shaving spread through all the Greek dominions.

24

Diogenes inspected haircuts and beards in search of manly bushy-haired men.

Women, more than men, aroused fury over hair in the ancient Roman Empire. By the start of the first century they had "a thousand styles of hairdressing," according to the poet Ovid, and they apparently tried them all at once: hair up, down, curled, pressed straight, towering over wire frames, bleached, dyed, or hidden under the gaudiest wigs they could find.

"While you are at home, your hair is at the hairdresser, who each morning brings you your eyebrows," the Roman writer Martial said

25

Various hair and wig styles of Roman ladies.

of one beauty. "Your charms are kept in a hundred different pots, and your face doesn't go to bed with you." In a wig-jeering mood, he penned:

> The golden hair that Galla wears
> Is hers—who would have thought it?
> She swears 'tis hers, and true she swears,
> For I know where she bought it.

In Rome, there were few natural blondes, so the state decided to make blonde hair a badge of sin. Wicked "ladies of the evening" were licensed, taxed, and required by law to dye their hair blonde or to wear yellow wigs. Valeria Messalina, third wife of Emperor Claudius, broke down both the law and the prejudice against blondes. She enjoyed putting on a yellow wig and sneaking out in the evening in the hope that men would take her to be one of the girls for hire.

Her disguise fooled hardly anybody, since she often lost her wig during the night and arrived back at the palace without it, and her own wickedness became the talk of Rome. But she also made yellow wigs fashionable, with an influence that seemed to have the same effect on Roman women as the slogan that was to come centuries later: "Blondes have more fun." To the outrage of Rome's self-appointed hair censors, respectable women rushed out to have their hair dyed blonde or to put on yellow wigs. Before long, Roman men complained they could no longer tell a lady from a tramp by the color of her hair.

Once the wig fashion started, there seemed no stopping it. Some wealthy women had several hundred wigs, not just yellow, but in various hues and styles. There were vain beauties who went so far as to have marble statues of themselves equipped with marble wigs, top pieces that fitted the heads of the statues like lids, so they could be changed to match

26

the changing styles of their own hair. Others washed their hair with bleaches of dried nuts and acid, hoping it would turn yellow, but sometimes found the acid turned them bald instead.

Juvenal, the Roman satirist, mocked women who swept the front of their hair up in curls over a wire frame, an *orbis,* until it was twice as high as their faces but almost vanished at the back of the neck in a tightly wound bun. He wrote that from the front women looked like the legendary heroine Andromache, but that they looked like nothing at all from behind:

> You'd think her life, or honor, was at stake,
> So high they pile her head, such tiers on tiers
> With wary hands they pile, that she appears
> Andromache before—and what behind?
> A dwarf, a creature of another kind.

Leaders of the new Christian religion took moral issue with the Empire's wig-wearing women. Church father Tertullian accused them of "annexing I know not what enormities of wigs and counterfeit hair." Clement of Alexandria said such women "deceive the men by the excessive quantity of their hair" and "defame the head, which is truly beautiful," and called it "a very wicked thing to attire the head with dead hair."

Some of Rome's balding older gentlemen wore wigs, which they curled, perfumed, and oiled. Others, to escape criticism for adopting "feminine attire," simply painted their bald heads black to imitate hair. Although they previously had worn their hair long, most men of the Roman Empire cut it short and cropped hair became the accepted style. Young dandies who let their hair grow a little long, or who curled the ends of it, were accused of making themselves look like women. Martial was among critics who mocked the sort of young rebel "who with the nicest care, in parted locks divides his curling hair."

Saint Paul, in one of his letters to the new Christian churches he founded, sent instructions intended to help quiet the growing dispute over whether men's hair should be long or short. By his time, close-cut hair was the prevailing custom, so in an epistle to the Corinthians (I Corinthians XI, 14:16), he wrote:

"Doth not even nature itself teach you, that, if a man have long hair, it is a shame unto him?" He added, however: "But if any man seem to be contentious, we have no such custom. . . ."

Those words, made part of the New Testament, were to be interpreted in various ways by centuries of Christian moralists, some of whom would judge the depth of a man's religion by the length of his hair.

A pioneering effort to introduce the razor to Rome reportedly was made in the 5th century B.C. by Tarquinus, one of the legendary early kings. But Romans at first resisted shaving, as an attempt to rob them of hairy manliness, and it was at least another century before a group of Greek barbers came from Sicily to set up shop in Rome.

Even then most Roman men merely had their beards trimmed and shortened, until a few daring individuals went all the way and had them entirely lopped off, much to the disapproval of their elders. But once the Romans discovered the pleasures of the barbershop it became the most popular place in town. Romans were the first to use warm water for shaving, and to make sure they got close shaves some had their chins rubbed with pumice stone.

From the beginning, according to Plutarch, men were annoyed by talkative barbers. He noted that the Roman general Archelaus was the first to make a remark other men would echo for years to come. When asked by one chattering barber how he would like his beard trimmed, Archelaus replied: "In silence."

Shaving was so customary by the time Cicero was delivering his orations in the 1st century B.C. that senators with "five-o'clock shadow" were turned away from the senate and refused their seats until they visited the barber. Caesar, it was said, went unshaven only once, during a vow to let his beard grow until he avenged a military defeat. Caligula, who became emperor in the year 37, sometimes wore a false beard of

The crowns of kings, according to legend, grew out of Julius Caesar's desire to conceal his baldness. His bald head reportedly inspired the Roman senate to grant him the right always to wear a laurel wreath crown, which set the pattern for crowns upon later royal heads.

Scipio Africanus, greatest general up to the time of Caesar, reportedly was the first Roman to shave daily. Shown here, clean-shaven among a group of bearded men, he and other military leaders set a fashion for shaving that caught on among civilians.

gold. Nero, who came to power about a decade later, made a public ceremony of dedicating his beard to the gods, presenting it at the temple in a small gold casket covered with jewels.

The clean-shaven look remained in style until Emperor Hadrian, the wall-builder, decided in the 2nd century A.D. that a wall of whiskers might help conceal the ugly battle scars on his face and the big wart on his chin. He hoped to make himself more presentable for public appearances in all parts of his far-flung Empire. For a time, that brought back beards, and men who shaved were called unpatriotic, although some braved the taunts and went right on shaving.

Emperors Antonius Pius and Marcus Aurelius also adopted Hadrian's bearded style. But Emperor Commodus, who found himself with so little to do that he spent his afternoons in his palace killing flies, revived the barbershops and restored the use of the razor. After his time Roman men shaved again for as long as the old Empire itself held together. During all the controversy over beards, Romans generally wore no moustaches, and continued to cut their hair short.

The clean-cut legionnaires who marched out of Rome to conquer the world also warred against long hair. All of Gaul, according to the Roman scholar Pliny, was "Hairy Gaul." Its men let their hair "fall down their necks . . . so thick it scarce differs from a horse's mane," historian Diodorus Siculus said, and they wore moustaches hanging over their mouths "so that when they eat and drink these brush their victuals or dip into their liquids." So conquering Caesar ordered the long hair of the conquered Gauls cut off.

LEFT Hadrian, who grew a beard to present a better face for public appearance tours. RIGHT Coin of Hadrian with full-grown beard.

Romans who later invaded Britain were startled to discover that natives there not only wore great moustaches "drooping like wings on their breasts," but also often dyed them vivid red, orange, green, or blue. Boadicea, Queen of the Britons, considered the Roman invaders "soft and unmanly" because they shaved, but to the advancing men of Rome the shave and haircut were the badge of civilization.

Beards, moustaches and long hair were the established habit of most barbarian tribes in Europe until the Romans, and then the Christian church, which had adopted Roman hair styles, wielded knife and razor. The Saxons had early laws to protect hair and beards, with heavy punishment for those who dared to barber a man against his will. Among the Franks, cutting a man's hair meant stripping him of noble rank, and to shave off a beard by force was as great a crime as cutting off an arm or leg.

When Charlemagne was King of the Franks he wore a long beard himself and warred with enemies who cut the beards off some of his men. But by the time he invaded Italy in the 8th century, on his way to becoming the first Holy Roman Emperor, he had acquired a properly Christian dislike for hairy heads and faces, and commanded all males in

30

A longhair of the Middle Ages, back and front view.

the Duchy of Benevento to shave. Later, when he was emperor, he reportedly grew his beard again, to add to the dignity of his appearance.

The split of the Roman Empire divided the world's hair. Western civilization gradually adopted the short-haired, clean-shaven look, while men in Eastern lands kept long hair and beards. In the East, Jews by long tradition were bearded. The rise of the Mohammedan religion also

Charlemagne with beard that he shaved off at times.

31

enforced reverence for beards, as millions of followers took oaths on the red beard of Mohammed, who told them to let their own beards grow so they would not be mistaken for shaven infidels.

When the Roman and Greek churches parted, there was another East-West parting of hair, with the Greeks keeping beards and a different design in the way the heads of priests were shaved. Monks and priests in the West had to shave their hair short, but even in Europe there were many churchly conflicts over proper tonsure. Christian moralists, determined to apply the shave and haircut not only to priests but to all men, waged battle through the Middle Ages against long hair and elaborate beards as a vanity that amounted to sin.

French priests succeeded so well that when William the Conqueror led his Normans into the Battle of Hastings in 1066 most of his men were beardless and had their hair shaved off the back of their necks to their ears. The opposing British, mostly bearded, wore hair to their shoulders, and legend has it that the difference in hair lengths contributed to the defeat of England's King Harold. His spies, so the story goes, spotted an advance group of Normans but because of their short-cropped hair took them to be a band of priests and failed to give proper warning of the invasion.

After he became the new King of England, William forced some of his British subjects to shave and cut their hair, and others adopted the Norman style as a matter of choice. But there were young men who resisted and the churchmen, alarmed by the regrowth of hair, exhorted as never before. Some threatened long-haired offenders with excommunication; others, like Bishop Wulstan of Worcester, took more direct action. The good bishop carried a knife up his sleeve. Whenever a long-haired penitent knelt to receive his blessing, Bishop Wulstan would whip out the knife, cut off a lock of the "criminal and beastly" hair, and throw it in the man's face.

Most of the men from all over Europe who joined in the Crusades to recover the Holy Land from the Saracens went off to the wars in the East with their hair short and faces shaved. But in the heat of battle some were too busy to shave and others imitated the hairy styles of their enemies. Many of the Crusaders returned to their homes in the West with their hair long and their beards full, to the outspoken disgust of stay-at-home Christians who accused long-haired Crusaders of copying the Saracen foes they had gone to holy war against. Despite all the church could do, beards and long hair came back into fashion for a time.

The Archbishop of Rouen warned that the very souls of those who wore their hair long would be in peril, even after death. Anselm, the

Archbishop of Canterbury, decreed that men's hair should be short enough to expose part of their ears. The churchmen were fighting not only fashion but the practical difficulty of shaving in an age when soap was not plentiful, and when a rough weekly razoring always left a bristly stubble on the chin.

It was because of the chin stubble that the romantic knights at the 12th century court of England's King Henry I gave up shaving. Led by the king himself, they decided to show consideration for the ladies and present softly bearded chins and gently moustached lips to the girls they kissed. Bishop Serlo denounced King Henry and his men for using their beards as such courtly ornaments of pleasure.

The bishop faced them in person and told them they had decked themselves out as Saracens to imitate the lust of "filthy goats." Their ringlets and intricately forked beards, he said, revealed "a deformity

West meets East in the four separate points of this fancy beard sported by a young longhair of the Middle Ages. His hair comes to a point at the center of his forehead in a very early version of what much later generations would call a Widow's Peak.

of the soul." His plea was so moving the king agreed to give up his locks. Bishop Serlo was a man prepared. He produced a pair of shears from his pocket and "publicly and in the sight of God" clipped off the king's hair and beard. He then finished the job by trimming the heads and chins of the leading nobles, and had them stamp their feet on their shorn hair to crush out the evil.

Women, too, began to show their hair, after years of having kept it under wraps because of constant churchly admonitions not to display themselves in any way that might unduly interest men. As knights became bolder, women found themselves upon a romantic pedestal, and made the most of it. Some dyed their hair blonde and lengthened it with false hair and ribbons. Once having let down their hair, they of course began to put it up, and by the 13th century were wearing it in large plaited horns that stuck out above each ear.

"If we do not get out of the way of the women," the Bishop of Paris preached, "we shall be killed, for they carry horns to kill men. They carry great masses of other people's hair on their heads."

Partly because a playful king got into a snowball fight, Europe's men of the 16th century cut their hair short, after letting it grow long for nearly a hundred years. It had been growing longer again all through

33

the century before, down over men's ears and then to their shoulders.

One snowy night in 1521, France's King Francis I, a monarch who greatly enjoyed royal pranks, armed himself and some of his knights with snowballs to bombard the home of a Count Montgomery in mock attack. During the romp someone threw a flaming torch instead of a snowball and it struck the king's head, burning him so badly it was necessary to shave off all his hair. His courtiers showed their sympathy by also shaving their heads. When the king's hair grew back, he kept it short, and so did they. Soon most of the fashionable young men of France were hurrying to the barber for a haircut in the style set by royalty.

What King Francis started in France became a royal command in England under the much-married King Henry VIII, who disposed of some of his wives by having them beheaded. His edict to the men of his realm was not "off with their heads" but "off with their hair." Henry was King of England at the time Francis ruled France and he took a liking to the new French hair style. Not content with the slow change of fashion, Henry had his own hair cut and put palace barbers to work trimming off the long hair of others.

The king "commanded all about his Court to poll their heads," according to Stow's *Annals* of 1535, "and to give them example, he caused his own head to be polled." As in France, lesser nobles and then com-

The king who snowballed a return to short hair, Francis I of France.

34

moners followed the royal lead. The longhairs, with two kings and the rush of fashion against them, were forced to surrender, and the average male haircut again became short, at first brushed forward from the crown and later brushed up stiffly from the forehead.

The pair of kings, while shortening hair on men's heads, encouraged the regrowth of beards. The snowball accident that cost the French king his hair also scarred his chin, so Francis I grew a beard to cover the scars, like Roman Emperor Hadrian long before him, and beards soon sprouted on other chins all over Europe. England's king, like most men of his time, had come to his throne clean-shaven, but when he issued his command against long hair on heads, he also ordered that from thenceforth his beard was "to be knotted and no more shaven." Henry VIII then grew a fine square-cut beard himself and bid his subjects to let their chin whiskers grow as they pleased.

But even with royal assent the right to beards was not regained without a struggle against an older generation that sternly opposed the return to facial shrubbery. Beards of the clergy were taxed in France, magistrates were forbidden to wear them, and some French judges ordered bearded men who appeared in court to shave before they would hear their cases. The Paris Parlement in 1536 refused to admit bearded men, and the Parlement of Rouen not only ordered members to shave but also to let their hair grow long.

In England, the clean-shaven town fathers of Canterbury in 1542 fined the sheriff and others for wearing beards. The same year in London, young practitioners of the law at Lincoln's Inn were not allowed to appear bearded in the dining hall. But the anti-beard faction was fighting a losing battle. A few years later Lincoln's Inn had to amend its rules to allow beards of up to two weeks' growth, and finally had to repeal the beard regulations entirely.

During Mary Tudor's brief reign as Queen of England an attempt was made to prevent commoners from wearing beards, by fining those with long whiskers, and when Queen Elizabeth took the throne in 1558 another effort was made to tax beards according to the social standing of their wearers. But the next year Elizabeth ordered all laws penalizing beards repealed and finally cleared the way for a crop of infinite variety.

The Elizabethan Age became a Bearded Age and few men, from Raleigh, Drake and Shakespeare to the least important, were without chin adornment. Seldom have men been so preoccupied with the growth of hair on their chins. With some, the amount of beard they could grow was their pride, but with the more fashionable, style and trim were vital. Many of the shapes to which they trimmed their beards were

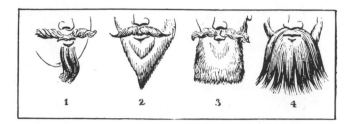

Some of the many styles returning beards took. 1. The "T" beard, or "Roman T." 2. "Stiletto." (A somewhat similar "Needle Beard" was narrowed and more pointed.) 3. The "Spade," especially popular with military men. 4. The "Cathedral," also known as "Broad Beard" and "Bishop's Beard."

fantastic. There were short, long, round, square, pointed, parted, narrow, and bushy beards; and French, Spanish, Dutch, and Italian cuts. Each style had a colorful name and there were endless variations in the croppings, twistings, and curlings.

Beards were powdered, waxed, drenched with perfume, and often dyed, red being a favorite color in compliment to sandy-haired Queen Elizabeth I. Men had little brushes to correct the slightest disorder of their beards, and some carried special combs to adjust their beards before or after dining. At night they encased their beards in cloth bags, or wore their chin hair clamped in wooden presses to avoid disarranging it while they slept. Poets and playwrights wrote of beards, and barbers reaped a hairy harvest.

As in ancient Rome, the barbershops of Europe again became social

The Barber, 1.
in the Barbers-ſhop, 2.
cutteth off the Hair
and the Beard
with a pair of Sizzars, 3.

Tonſor, 1.
in Tonſtrina, 2.
tondet Crines
& Barbam
Forcipe, 3.

Early English barbershop, as pictured in one of the first illustrated schoolbooks, *Orbis Pictus* or *Visible World,* published in the 1600s to teach Latin. At the left of the text are explanations in English; at the right, is the Latin equivalent. In those days barbers were still surgeons who pulled teeth and let blood as well as trimming beards and cutting hair. The traditional striped barber's pole which later stood in front of many shops came from the one a man gripped with his hands during minor surgery. The stripes symbolized bandages hung on it to dry.

clubs, where some men spent most of the day. Shops had caged song-birds to entertain customers and they also provided musical instruments so that men waiting their turn could join in song when they weren't exchanging gossip or criticizing each other's beards.

Sixteenth century man's adoration of his own beard brought the hair moralists out in full cry. Even when heads were falling and men were being burned at the stake in the conflicts between the Roman Catholic Church and new Protestants, the Christian clergy found time to denounce beards. Since many of the churchmen wore beards themselves the chin whiskers had their defenders as well as attackers, with men on each side quoting the Bible for or against beards. Martyred Protestant Bishop John Hooper, before being put to death in 1555, warned that excessive beards were causes of idleness. The average young dandy took as long to set his beard, the bishop charged, as a craftsman took to produce a useful length of cloth.

Pamphleteer Philip Stubbes, the Puritan whose *The Anatomie of Abuses* was a best seller which ran through three editions in the 1580s, warned that barbers had developed a "monstrous manner" of cutting and trimming beards. Among them he listed "one the new cut, another the old; one the gentleman's cut, another the common cut; one the cut of the court, another of the country; with infinite and like varieties which I overpasse." When a man went to get his beard trimmed, Stubbes said, the barber asked "whether you will be cut to look terrible to your enemy or amiable to your friend."

In an age when beards were so admired some men gained passing fame for the length of theirs. An unfortunate longbeard was Hans Steininger, chief magistrate of Braunau, Austria. His beard was eight feet, nine inches long. In order to walk around he had to wrap it about his neck and tuck it up across his chest. On his way to a council meeting on September 28, 1567, the burgomaster's beard slipped its moorings. He tripped over the end of it, fell down the stairs, and was killed.

Women began the 16th century with their hair modestly hidden from male view, but a flowering of feminine hair soon had moralists as alarmed as they were over masculine beards. Italian women were the first to rediscover their hair, and Frenchwomen soon bared their hair, too. In England, women more timidly did it by degrees, wearing hoods that grew smaller and smaller, until fashion finally replaced them with little bonnets which left almost all the hair on their heads exposed.

Italian noblewoman Catherine de' Medici, who became Queen of France in 1547, frizzed her hair out over pads and wire frames that held it in puffs at the temples, and fashionable women elsewhere followed

Catherine de' Medici

her lead. They began adding false curls and ringlets and a fad for building artificial and elaborate hair-dos grew, along with a craze that made almost every dark-haired woman want to be a blonde.

Some, more romantic than practical, were convinced that brushing their hair by moonlight might help turn it from black to yellow. But wealthy women in Italy had sun turrets, small wooden huts, built on the roofs of their homes, where they could sit to bleach. "They repair to these boxes and condemn themselves to broil in them," painter Cesare Vecelli complained in 1589, as "they keep wetting their hair with a sponge dipped in some elixir of youth."

Hair became so complicated to arrange, and such a nuisance to dye, that many women simply cut it off and put on wigs. By mid-century the wig was an indispensable part of every fashionable lady's wardrobe.

Queen Elizabeth I covered the head from which she had shaved her thinning sandy hair with red wigs, and had more than eighty of them in different styles. Her ill-fated rival, Mary Queen of Scots, had at least as many wigs as Elizabeth. Even in prison, Mary changed her wig almost every day, and wore her favorite to the executioner's block.

Philip Stubbes, so critical of men's beards, felt called upon to issue a Christian warning to women as well. With their wigs and dyed locks adorned with jewels, pearls and feathers, he held that they were forgetting woman's humble role in society and were making their hair "an ornament of pride, and destrouction to themselves for ever, excepte they repent."

The way women were "trimming and tricking their heades" and "laying out their haire to shewe," propped with "forks, wiers, and I cannot tell what, like grim sterne monsters," was a scandal to Stubbes. But what he considered "devilish and more than thrise cursed" was that "not simplie content with their own haire, they buye other haire, either of horses, mares or any other straunge beastes" and fashion it into wigs.

Despite Stubbes and other critics, most women appeared willing to take their chances. And men, by then not content with mere beards, began to let the hair on their heads grow longer again, perhaps in envy of all the attention women were getting. By 1590 the fashion of short hair for men had passed its peak. With some exceptions of time and place, men were about to go hairy again for two hundred years to come, but not always with hair of their own.

Young King Louis XIII of France never was able to grow much of a beard and was somewhat jealous of the better beards his nobles grew. They copied his style in most things but were reluctant to shave their beards to match the king's. One day in 1628 the king decided to amuse himself by playing barber. He took up soap and razor and personally

LEFT Louis XIII, when he was long-haired, moustached, and had about as much beard as he was able to grow. RIGHT After he gave up the beard, and replaced his hair with a wig. *Picture Collection, New York Public Library*

shaved his courtiers, sparing only their moustaches and a tiny tuft of hair on each chin.

From that day, the beard was doomed. Whatever was done at the elegant French court was fashion almost everywhere in Europe. The beard struggled on for a time, short and curly or trimmed and pointed, and the moustache, stiffly waxed to a pencil line of hair, lasted even longer. But the trend toward another clean-shaven age had begun.

As hair vanished from men's faces, it grew longer on their heads. What Louis XIII lacked on his chin, he made up for with a luxurious crop of hair. But while he was still in his twenties he started to go prematurely bald. To cover his embarrassment, he donned a wig, and his courtiers, to ease the king's feelings, also wore wigs. It wasn't until somewhat later that wig wearing became a necessity among fashionable men, but the royal nod had been given to another trend.

The beauty of men's long hair was so admired that one of the leaders of fashion, the Seigneur de Cadenet, reportedly was made a French marshal by King Louis XIII, instead of his older brother, because his hair was prettier. He wore one separate blond lock, tied with a bow of ribbon, hanging over his left shoulder. A pearl earring dangled from his exposed left ear. With or without the earring, that became the craze of young men. In France the hanging lock was called a *cadenette*. Among English dandies it was known as a *lovelock* or *earlock*. Some men, not content with one, wore as many as six lovelocks, each a curl longer than the rest of their hair.

To the growing Puritan sect in England hair became a political as well as a religious issue. And among Puritan leaders who considered long hair and lovelocks not only a matter of royal decadence but a sin against God, none was more fanatic than William Prynne. In 1628, the same year Louis XIII was barbering his nobles, Prynne wrote a sixty-three-page diatribe that was to be a text for haters of long hair for years to come.

When Prynne penned *The Unloveliness of Lovelocks* he was twenty-eight, a beginning lawyer who had just been admitted to the bar at

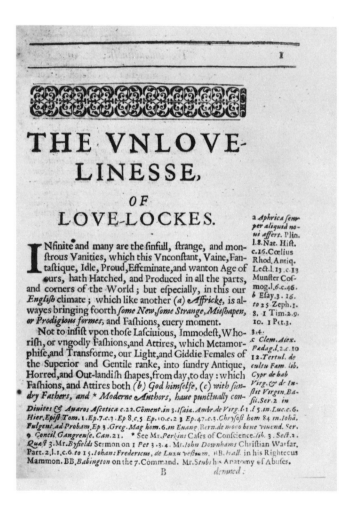

The first of William Prynne's sixty-three pages of denunciation of long hair and lovelocks, published in 1628, which began, "Infinite and many are the sinfull, strange, and monstrous Vanities, which this . . . wanton Age of ours hath Hatched." *Beinecke Rare Book and Manuscript Library, Yale University*

40

Lincoln's Inn. He quoted warnings of church authorities from early New Testament times and denounced "the Sinfull and Unmanly Crisping, Curling, Frouncing, powdring and nourishing of Lockes and Haire excrements" as evil, dangerous, depraving, indecent, lascivious, ruffianly, slothful, wanton, and wasteful, among other things.

It was bad enough, Prynne held, that women were being "transformed into men" by vain fashions that made them forget their "subjection both to God and man," but far more odious that "divers of our masculine and more noble race are wholly degenerated . . . into women" by "the very length and Culture of their Lockes and Haire," which he considered a "badge of . . . Vanitie, Singularitie and Effeminacy." The barber had become men's chaplain and his "shop their Chappell, their God," he accused, and long hair was "a deformitie that must needs taxe God's Judgement."

As one of the leaders of the forces of Parliament in its battles against King Charles I, Prynne was imprisoned for writing such pamphlets, including one questioning the morals of the queen herself, and was punished as a "seditious libeler" by having his ears cut off. Freed by Parliament after the Civil War that overthrew the king, he became a prosecutor of royalists, and lived to see King Charles I beheaded, although he had no part in that.

Hair nevertheless divided the two forces in the Civil War. The king's cavaliers had locks that tumbled in bouncy ringlets to their shoulders, but most of the Puritans and other Parliamentarians who fought the King's Men had haircuts that looked as if a bowl had been plopped on their heads and the edges trimmed around it. That was partly a matter of religious scruples, but also because their ranks included tradesmen and poorer people who couldn't afford the fancy hair styling of the wealthy. The round haircuts earned Puritans the nickname of Roundheads.

Thomas Hall, the good pastor of Kingsnorton, came back to the attack on hair in 1653 with a book twice as long as Prynne's. His *Comarum, The Loathsomnesse of Long Hair* promised to prove not only that the "judgement of Divines both old and new" was that "it is unlawfull for any man ordinarily to weare Long Haire," but also to set proper limits as to just "when may wee say that a man's Haire is too long."

It was too long, he said, when men require "Strings or fillets to tie up their Haire that it fall not in their eyes when they worke" and " 'tis excessive when it is so long it covers the eyes, the cheeks, the countenance . . . since the haire of the head is ordeined by God for the covering of the head, not the face." It should not be allowed to grow to any length "scandalous and offensive," he cautioned, "so that the godly are thereby

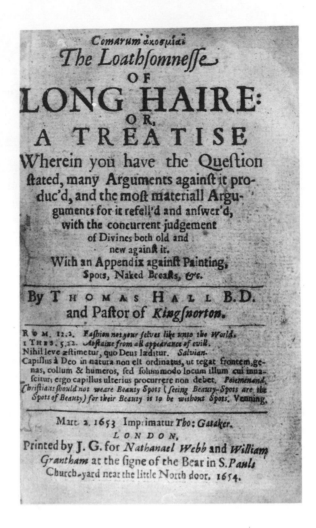

Comarum ἀκοσμιαι
The Loathsomnesse
OF
LONG HAIRE:
OR,
A TREATISE
Wherein you have the Question
stated, many Arguments against it pro-
duc'd, and the most materiall Argu-
guments for it refell'd and answer'd,
with the concurrent judgement
of Divines both old and
new against it.
With an Appendix against Painting,
Spots, Naked Breasts, &c.

By THOMAS HALL B.D.
and Pastor of *Kingsnorton.*

RoM. 12.2. *Fashion not your selves like unto the World.*
1 THES. 5.22. *Abstaine from all appearance of evill.*
Nihil leve æstimetur, quo Deus læditur. *Salvian.*
Capillus à Deo in natura non est ordinatus, ut tegat frontem, ge-
nas, collum & humeros, sed solummodo locum illum cui inna-
scitur, ergo capillus ulterius procurrere non debet. *Poimenend.*
*Christians should not weare Beauty Spots (seeing Beauty-Spots are the
Spots of Beauty) for their Beauty is to be without Spots.* Venning.

Mart. 2. 1653 Imprimatur *Tho: Gataker.*
LONDON,
Printed by J. G. for *Nathanael Webb* and *William*
Grantham at the signe of the Bear in S. *Pauls*
Church-yard near the little North door. 1654.

Beinecke Rare Book and Manuscript Library, Yale University

grieved, the weak offended, and the wicked hardened" or "when it is contrary to the civil and laudable custome of those civiliz'd Nations which we live in."

Just in case anybody still had doubts, Hall summed it up: "It is clear that long Haire is one of the sinfull customes and fashion of the wicked men of the world." Waxing poetic, he urged:

> Go, Gallants, to the Barbers, go.
> Bid them your hairy Bushes mow.
> God in a Bush did once appeare,
> But there is nothing of Him here.

While men of England were still arguing over the length of hair, and warring over whether to have a kingdom, a commonwealth, or a military dictatorship, their future King Charles II was in exile at the

42

court of France's King Louis XIV, and men there already had shaved off their hair to put on wigs.

Male hair was enthroned in splendor at the court of Louis XIV, the long-haired Sun King, to whom fashion leadership was part of the glory of France, and also a calculated means of establishing his image as the most magnificent of world rulers. He removed his nobles from their own estates and gathered them around himself at glittering Versailles, to occupy them in the pursuit of fashion where they would be no threat to his personal power. When he declared, "I am the state," he also was declaring, "I am the fashion." He remained the arbiter of Europe's hair through the longest reign of any monarch until his time.

Louis XIV at first disdained the wigs that had been growing in use since his father, Louis XIII, introduced them. He made his natural hair supreme over that of his shaven nobles whose wigs could only imitate his God-given hair. But when he discovered signs of coming baldness, he at last gave in, had his head shaved, and took to wearing a variety of wigs. Forty wigmakers were needed to meet the king's demand and a private corridor of the palace was fitted with stands to hold his wigs.

His personal barber, Binette, who shaved his head every day was the only one ever allowed to see Louis XIV bald. At night when the

LEFT   Louis XIV, while still wearing mostly his own hair, and with what was left of the moustache.   RIGHT   With full wig in place of his hair, after giving the *coup de grâce* to the moustache.

Only his big wig and royal attire made the king in this caricature, which was sketched a century after Louis XIV's death by writer and artist William Makepeace Thackeray, best known as the author of *Vanity Fair*. At the left is the king's empty wig and raiment; in the center the king as he looked without it; and at the right, wig and man put together. "You see at once, that majesty is made out of the wig," Thackeray wrote. "Thus do barbers . . . make the gods we worship."

king retired, the curtains of his bed were drawn around him before he passed out his wig to a waiting page, and in the morning a casual wig to wear while dressing was passed in through the curtains before the king got out of bed. Once Louis XIV adopted the wig, the fashion was set, not only in France but in most of Europe.

Louis XIV also gave the *coup de grâce* to moustaches. Beards already were vanishing and moustaches had become a shred. When the king discovered tell-tale white hairs in his lip whiskers, he had his moustache shaved off to eliminate the offending truth of age. His nobles scurried to their barbers, and many gentlemen in other lands also put the razor to the last hairs on their faces as soon as they got the word from Paris.

Meanwhile Charles II had been restored to England's throne and soon after he returned from exile at the French court he appeared wearing a huge full-bottomed wig. He was the first English king to wear a wig and English gentlemen, some of whom had flirted with the fashion even before his restoration, adopted the kingly style.

Wigs became both common and complicated, so that technical descriptions of their styles and parts required pages of published definition. One lengthy treatise by Randle Holme, describing various wigs in use, explained that "a Perawicke . . . is counterfeit hair which men wear

44

instead of their own, a thing much used in our days . . . contrary to our forefathers, who got Estates, loved their Wives, and wore their own hair."

Samuel Pepys, whose diary was to provide future generations with a lively view of life in 17th century England, was as troubled by the shift from hair to wigs as most men. Along with others, he called them *perukes,* then *periwigs*. The word came from the French *perruque,* which originally meant a head of hair, then of false hair. The English, through mispronunciation and at least two dozen different spellings, converted that to *perwyke,* then *perriwigg,* and finally dropped the first part and just called the thing a *wig*.

Pepys first dallied with the idea of wearing a wig in the spring of 1663 when he visited "Jervas, my old barber" and "did try on two or three periwigs . . . meaning to wear one; and yet I have no stomach for it." But that November, "Chapman, the periwigg-maker" brought one to his house that he approved and "without more ado . . . he cut off my hairc, which went a little to my heart at present to part with it; but it being over, and my periwigg on . . . I caused all my maids to look upon it, and they concluded it do become me."

Among Puritans and other reform groups there was as much fury against the new wigs as there had been against unlovely lovelocks and loathsome long hair. Some churches were so hostile to wigs that they turned wearers away from the door, and there were some outraged

King Charles II

45

Samuel Pepys, with long wig he was reluctant to wear at first, but came to like. *Picture Collection, New York Public Library*

vestrymen who ripped wigs from the heads of offending ministers. In rural areas, there were near-riots over wig-wearing.

Other hair critics attacked wigs more with laughter than rage. *The Weekly Comedy* in 1690 likened the face of a bewigged man to a calf peeping out of a thicket of brambles, and another satirist called the face of a fashionably wigged gentleman "a small pimple in the midst of a vast sea of hair." *Westminster Drollery* published a poem in which a girl told a young man:

> Ask me no more where all the day
> The foolish Owl doth make her stay:
> 'Tis in your locks; for tak't from me,
> She thinks your hair an Ivy tree.

Pocket combs, some of gold or silver and handsomely jeweled, became conversation pieces for fashionable young men who endlessly combed their wigs in public dining halls, at the theater, while gathered in the park to watch the girls go by, and while gossiping together in drawing rooms.

With a wig bigger than his hat, this 17th century man defies both ridicule and winter weather, his hands in a muff.

46

Some also began to powder their wigs with flour, and to make the powder stick they had to coat them with gummy perfumed pomade. A writer of *Wit's Recreations* ridiculed the "powder-wig" who "like a pageant doth walk the street," in a jingle that ended:

> See how his perfumed head is powdered o'er;
> 'Twould stink else, for it wanted salt before.

Not all 17th century men wore wigs, as almost all men would in the century to come. Many still preferred their own hair and more could not afford a wig. Large wigs, worth an average tradesman's earnings for a year, often were willed by a dying man to some fortunate heir. Wigs were a barrier that divided the wealthy from the middle class. Without one a man could hardly hope to be accepted in the company of gentlemen.

France's Louis XIV, who had changed the hair of Europe's men, also lifted women's hair into artificial towers, more by accident than design. His teen-aged mistress, Marie, the Duchesse de Fontanges, was on a

Duchesse de Fontanges, teen-aged favorite of Louis XIV, who put a garter around her head and lifted women's hair to new heights. *Picture Collection, New York Public Library*

royal hunting party one day when her hair tumbled down. She pulled a garter from her leg, fastened it over her hair, and the king was so obviously pleased that other ladies of the court rushed to their hairdressers to achieve the same effect.

Poor Marie died when she was twenty, but the hair style she had accidentally created lived on for some thirty years as a *fontange,* much to the later disgust of the king, who became thoroughly sick of it and said so. Women in France, England, and almost everywhere else took their cue from Paris. They replaced Marie's simple style of a plain band

47

around the hair with capped arrangements of linen and lace, topped by palisades of hair, most of it false.

Arrayed over pads and wire frames, the hair climbed and spread in battlements of curls, one row atop the other. Each cascading curl had a poetic French name. Small curls in a fringe on the forehead were *cruches;* ringlets dangling at the sides of the face were *favourites;* little curls at the ears were *confidants;* tiny curls at the nape of the neck were *crève-coeurs* or *heart-breakers.*

The anti-hair moralists, having all but given up the lost battle against men's wigs, rose in a unity of rage to meet the new feminine challenge. They denounced women for making their hair "tours of vanitie" that would "tempt Lucifer's selfe," and accused barbers who catered to such fashions of running "devill's shopps."

Peter the Great of Russia became history's greatest mass persecutor of beards as the 17th century ended. By tradition and for religious reasons most Russian men had kept beards long after the rest of the men of Europe had shaved theirs off. As part of his campaign to Westernize his empire, Peter decided to tax beards and moustaches out of existence.

LEFT Russian folk drawing showing one of the tax agents of Peter the Great removing an unlicensed beard.

BELOW Tax token that licensed Russian beards.

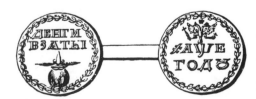

Tax collectors, armed with scissors, were stationed at the gates of every city and others roamed the rural provinces to crop the beards and moustaches of those who refused to pay the tax. Nobles and wealthy merchants had to pay one hundred roubles a year to continue wearing beard or moustache. The tax for others was scaled according to rank, down to only one kopeck for peasants.

Those who decided it was worth the price were given a brass token, called *borodoràia* ("the bearded"), as a tax receipt, which was a one-year license to go bearded or moustached. On the face of the token was a nose, mouth, moustache, and flowing beard, along with Russian words for "money received." The reverse side gave the year and pictured the Black Eagle of empire. It had to be shown on demand and those who couldn't produce one risked having beards scissored on the spot. Defiant wearers of illegal beards were arrested and imprisoned at hard labor. Peter the Great and his successors carried on the taxing and cutting of Russian beards for almost half a century.

Captain John Smith

When hairy young Captain John Smith and others came from England early in the 17th century to establish the first permanent North American colony in what was to be Virginia, he discovered in his dealings with the Indians around Jamestown that long hair was a native American birthright. The Powhatans wore their hair not only long, but braided, usually in one braid for the men and two for the women.

That news from America deeply disturbed the anti-hair moralists back in London. Pastor Thomas Hall of Kingsnorton held the Indians of Virginia up to good English Christians as a horrible example of "the Loathsomnesse of Long Haire." A look at the customs in such "remote parts of the world," he said, would show "that long haire was . . . the guise and fashion of the most barbarous, idolatrous, heathenish Nations that know not God but worshippe the Devill, as the Virginians in America, to whom the Devill appeares in the shape of a Virginian, with a long black lock on the left side hanging down to neere the feete, whom the Virginians imitate in this Devillish Guise."

But the English settlers who came to Virginia, more Cavalier than Roundhead, had few scruples themselves about long hair, since their own was long, ringleted, and curled. Unlike the Indians, the English Virginians did wear beards, chin tufts that were neatly trimmed and carefully styled, and they were eager followers of the hair fashion news brought by each ship arriving from home. When beards finally vanished in Europe, as they soon would, most of the immigrants in Virginia became as clean-shaven as the natives.

Up in Massachusetts the Pilgrims who came poor from Holland to land at Plymouth, and the richer Puritans who came from England to settle around Boston and Salem, brought to the New World the hair prejudices they had nourished in the old. As early as 1634 the Massachusetts legislature passed a law which forbade long hair "if uncomely or prejudicial to the common good."

Strict John Endecott, when governor in 1649, tried to put through a more drastic law. But not all Puritans felt as he did and the law was rejected. Endecott and eight other leaders then issued a manifesto of their own to declare their "detestation against the wearing of such long hair, as against a thing uncivil and unmanly, whereby men doe deforme themselves." They earnestly pleaded with all elders "to manifest their zeal against it in their public administrations."

John Endecott, a leader of America's first crusade against long hair.

How long hair could be before it was too long became a burning issue. Endecott himself had hair that reached his shoulders and at least four other signers of his plea wore their hair over their ears. Deputy Governor Thomas Dudley, among those who issued the manifesto, thought hair could be "worne . . . without offense to the godly" if "the haire cover the hole of the ear and nape of the necke."

Some blamed the young men at Harvard College, "brought up in such pride as doth no wayes become such," for infecting others with the

50

desire for long hair "which lust first took head and brake out at the Colledg . . . to the great griefe and offence of many godly hearts." When Harvard made an appeal for contributions, a group of citizens answered with a petition complaining that the college youth did not show an attitude of proper "mortification and humility" toward their elders, as was evident from the way their "haires . . . are defiled."

John Eliot, missionary to the Indians, inspired the petition against the "savage hair" of Harvard men. He was then nearly seventy, and the rest of the petitioners definitely were of the older generation, one a man in his nineties. "We beseech you consider," they beseeched, "whether all other lusts which have so incorigibly brake in upon our youth have not first sprung from the incoriagableness of this lust."

John Eliot *Picture Collection, New York Public Library*

Eliot had a "boiling zeal" against men who wore their hair "with a Luxurious, Delicate, Feminine Prolixity" and who preserved "no plain distinction of their Sex by the Hair of their head and face" and he was doubly concerned because the hair styles he blamed on the Harvard men "now is got into our pulpets" so that some young ministers seemed tempted to "ruffle it in Excess of this kind."

He and other hair fanatics in New England were echoing a campaign going on in old England at about the same time against the long hair of university students there. Cambridge, Massachusetts, where Harvard was, had been so named by some of its founders who were graduates of old Cambridge University in England, where long hair was forbidden in 1636. An irate professor at Cambridge University had seized one student and cut off his hair with a bread knife, holding him down on the buttery hatch while he performed the operation. Oxford, too, threatened to expel students who wore hair "indecently long."

So Harvard, in the spring of 1655, issued a rule that it should not "bee lawfull for any to weare Long haire, Locks or foretops" or "to use Curling, Crisping, Parting or Powdering." Harvard President Charles Chauncy devoted most of his commencement sermon to explaining the rule in detail. He quoted the Bible to prove that "the Lord hath forbidden unto men long hair," which meant "cutting of the hair short and all locks . . . and to nourish any part thereof is contrary to the word of God." To students who still wondered how short was too long, Harvard's president said it would be wise to "make choise of the surer part" because "short hair we may be sure will neither offend God nor good men, but long hair may and doth offend both."

Wigs were not in style when the first colonial settlers left England for America, but as soon as they became the fashion in Europe they appeared in the colonies. New Englanders first considered them both an eyesore and a sin, but colonial gentlemen with close connections in England soon were wearing wigs just as large, as costly, and as well-powdered as those worn by Englishmen.

Clergymen stormed from their pulpits against them. Increase Mather warned his Boston congregation that wigs were "Horrid Bushes of Vanity . . . contrary to the Light of Nature and to express Scripture." The Reverend George Weeks accused Boston wig-wearers of being "sickly, weakly, crazy Persons," and said that "the monstrous Periwigs such as some of our church members indulge in make them resemble the locusts that came out of the Bottomless Pit."

Missionary John Eliot was convinced the terrible Indian uprising of 1675 was a vengeance of God against the wickedness of wearing wigs. The horror of King Philip's War, he believed, was God's direct punishment of the people because they "disfigure themselves with hair that is None of their own," which was an "abomination unseemlie in the sight of God."

Probably the greatest foe of long hair and wigs in all the colonies was

The first wigs that came from England to New England were long-haired.

LEFT Judge Samuel Sewell. RIGHT Cotton Mather. *Picture Collection, New York Public Library*

Judge Samuel Sewall, the Chief Justice of Massachusetts and a judge of the Salem witchcraft trials. Sewall devoted a good part of his life to fighting against "the unutterable peril" of wigs as "godless emblems of iniquity," and in his diary wrote a day-to-day account of his war against them. His greatest praise for a friend who had died was that "he was a true New-English man and abominated Periwigs." When a Boston wigmaker died a drunkard, Sewall noted in his diary, with melancholy satisfaction, that "this day Wm. Clendon the . . . Perriwig-maker, dies miserably, being almost eat up with lice and stupified with Drink and cold."

Boston's leading clergyman, Cotton Mather, had a tolerant attitude toward hair and wigs, unlike his father Increase Mather. A handsome and somewhat vain man, he adopted a very stylish full-bottomed wig himself, and took to his pulpit one Sunday to preach against wig-haters "who strained at a gnat and swallowed a camel." Cotton Mather called them hypocrites for being so "zealous against an innocent fashion taken up and used by the best of men."

Samuel Sewall thought Mather's remarks were rather pointedly directed toward him and complained that "I expected not to hear a vindication of Perriwiggs in Boston pulpit by Mr. Mather." But Mather reasoned that it was "lawful" for Christians to "accomodate the length of our hair unto the modest Customs which vary in the Churches of God."

53

Even without hair of their own, wig-wearing Europeans of the 18th century went right on quarreling over the length of it. In an age of revolution against the establishment, which was to see royalty overthrown in France as well as in America, young men found the big wigs of their elders revolting. But they tried hundreds of different ways of wearing false hair before they finally gave up the wig.

Full bottomed wigs had grown so big at the start of the century that some cascaded in false ringlets almost to a man's waist and covered his shoulders like a shawl. Critics of the long-haired wigs poked fun at them in pictures, verse, and plays.

Judge's wig

Tired of such blankets of hair, young rebels of fashion lowered and shortened their wigs, so that by 1730 the big ones were out of style, although older and conservative men still wore them. In some professions big wigs lingered for years, even down to the present day on the heads of England's judges. But as wigs became smaller, they also became more numerous, so that soon there were hundreds of varieties, and tradesmen and laborers as well as the rich and noble took to wearing them, until hardly any man was without a wig. As satirist Peter Pindar wrote:

Those wigs, which once were worn alone by kings,
Whence they derived their air of awful state,
Now decorated every plebeian pate . . .

Wigs were "as essential to every person's head as lace is to their clothes," the *London Chronicle* commented in 1726, but went on to criticize the new rage for wigs that made many men look like the rows of pots displayed on drugstore shelves "which are much ornamented but always stand empty." Never before had men worn their hair in so many styles at once, changing it as often and as quickly as they wished, limited only by the number of wigs any man could afford. With so much false hair on their heads, men's beards and moustaches vanished almost completely.

Pigtails were the first innovation that divided the century wig wearers. Soldiers and sailors started sweeping their hair out of the way to bunch the curls together at the back and tie them with black ribbon. Sometimes their queues were braided or stiffened with pipe clay or tar. Before long, military wigs had detachable queues, some of hair and others of wood, whalebone, leather or wire, with little tufts of real hair at the end.

Bag wigs, also adopted by civilians from the military, may have started because horses' tails often were covered with protective bags, fastened at the top with drawstrings, to protect their clothes from the

54

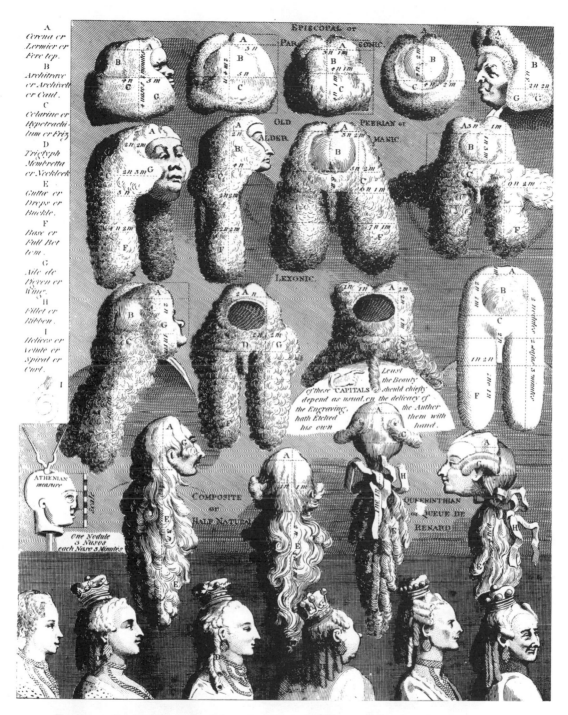

English artist William Hogarth poked fun at huge periwigs by picturing them in terms of precise architectural measurement, mocking their formality, in what was to become one of his better-known engravings, *The Five Orders of Perriwigs*, 1761. Even by then they were considered old-fashioned. Most men had turned to short-haired wigs, at least shorter than these. *Prints Division, The New York Public Library, Astor, Lenox and Tilden Foundations*

grease and general filth of their hair, and fashion made the bagged queues popular in a variety of wig styles.

The bewildering maze of wigs generally could be divided into two main groups, those with queues and those without them, and each had its critics and defenders.

LEFT   Pigtail looped.   RIGHT   Bag wig.

Wigmaker's shop in 18th century France, from an engraving by Charles Nicholas Cochin. At left, partly under the drape, one worker combs hair for a wig in the hackle, while another sits with a wig block on his lap, sewing weft. At table in front of window, woman is weaving strands of hair on a frame. Man standing at left, facing window, is powdering the wig on his head. In center, a seated customer is having his chin as well as his head shaved by an apprentice. Two workers at the back are heating curling irons in the fire. The apprentice at the right is dressing a wig. Hanging on rear wall are wigs of various styles.

56

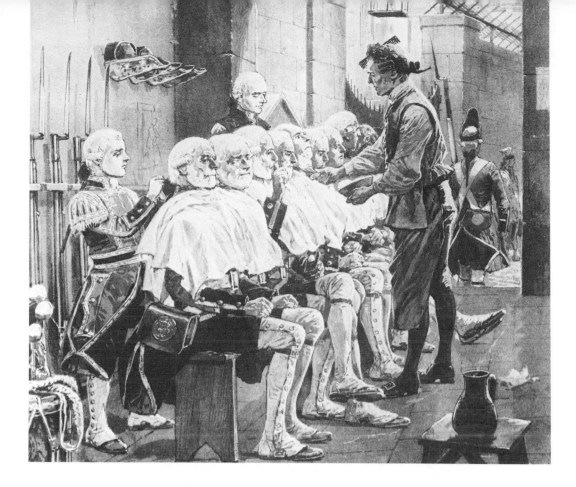

Production-line wig dressing and barbering in reality. British soldiers of the 18th century, awaiting turn to go on guard duty, get a wholesale shave and wig-fix. The drummer-boy at rear is tying ribbons to their queues.

Wigmakers advertised short bobs, long bobs, tie wigs, bag wigs, tuck-up wigs, naturals, half-naturals, and a long list of others, including "Grecian flyes, Curley Roys, Airy Levants." Some offered such added inducements as beer served on the premises or delivered to homes where wigs were to be fitted and dressed. Wigs were curled over hot clay pipes, doctored with special tools, carried in boxes designed to preserve their form, hung in rows on stands topped by wooden heads.

Big cities had hundreds of wigmakers; small towns from two to a dozen, and the craft became an art that produced detailed books of instruction and styling. One London advertiser promised wigs that would give clergymen "a certain demure, sanctified air," claimed that those he offered lawyers provided "an appearance of great sagacity and deep penetration," that professional men could be supplied with wigs of "solemnity and gravity," and that his military wigs would give the wearers "a most warlike fierceness."

57

Production-line wig dressing and barbering as suggested by an 18th century
English caricaturist, who humorously foresaw a horse-powered automatic
barbershop which could "shave sixty men a minute, also oyl, comb and

58

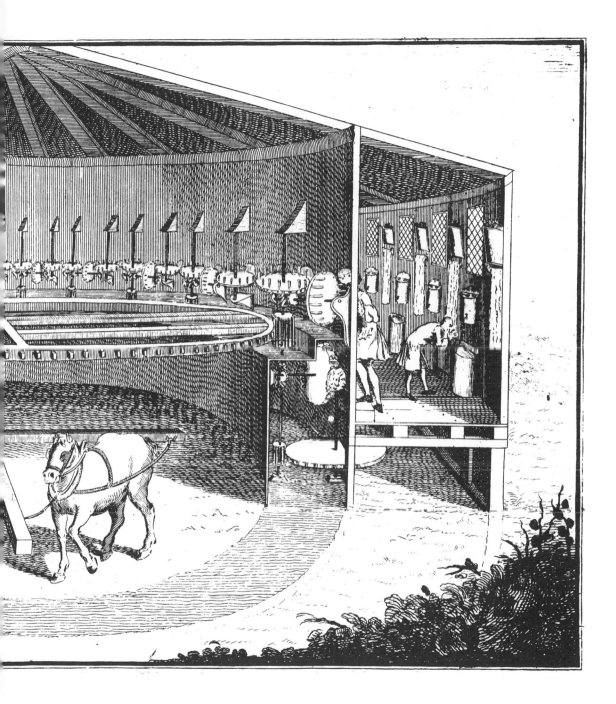

powder their wigs." Note wig being combed on revolving stand at lower right.
Prints Division, The New York Public Library, Astor, Lenox and Tilden Foundations

While the cat, with fascination, looks down upon the strange habits of humans, a servant holding a bag of wig powder shakes it over the wig and person who is using a face cone to keep from suffocating. In the 18th century, a powder room really was a *powder* room.

For a good part of the century wig powdering was considered so vital that soldiers powdered each other's queues in barracks, commoners suffered through the ordeal in attic closets or in barbershops, and wealthy people in London and Paris built their homes to provide special rooms for powdering.

When he sat for powdering, the person wore his wig liberally smeared with sticky grease, wrapped himself in a cloth or robe to cover his whole body except for his head, and buried his nose in a face-shielding cone made of paper or glass to try to keep from suffocating in the dust dumped upon him or pumped from a hand bellows. The rich used scented powders, usually white, although some men preferred blue or violet, and the poor used plain flour, pounds of it at a time.

Sometimes the powder was pumped directly at the wigged head, and sometimes squirted up at the ceiling so it would fall in gentler clouds to spread its color more naturally. Despite the sticky wigs, the powder

60

rubbed off to stain clothes, flaked on shoulders like dandruff, and men who overpowered left trails of it in the air wherever they walked. As John Gay advised in his poem, *Trivia,* in 1716:

> Him like the Miller, pass with caution by,
> Lest from his shoulder clouds of powder fly.

Gay, a poet and playwright who was a frequent critic of hair fashions, also called attention to the fact that wigs had tempted thieves into a profitable new form of crime. Stealing them had become common, and he poetically described the ingenious method pictured here:

> Nor is the wig with safety worn;
> High on the shoulder, in a basket borne,
> Lurkes the small boy, whose hand to rapine bred,
> Plucks off the curling honours of thy head.

Wig thieves sometimes worked in pairs: one would bump into a man in a crowd while another snatched his wig from behind and tossed it to a dog trained to run off with it. Wig-wearing gentlemen were not safe even riding in hackney coaches at night, the *London Weekly Journal* reported in 1717, because thieves would slash a hole right through the back of a coach to steal the wig off a passenger's head. The newspaper cautioned men to "sit in the fore seat, which will prevent that way of robbing."

By 1765 many of London's young men had given up wigs for natural hair. Wigmakers, many of them thrown out of work, staged a demonstration by marching through the streets to the palace. They presented a petition to King George, asking him to force all adult males to wear wigs by royal edict. But a lot of the protesting wigmakers wore no wigs themselves and a London mob hooted that the demand was unfair. There was a street brawl that turned to riot. Some of the defenders of natural hair got up a petition of their own, mocking the one presented by the wigmakers. Claiming to represent wooden leg makers, they slyly petitioned the king to have one of his legs removed and to wear a wooden leg that would promote their trade. The king got the joke and denied both petitions.

The natural hair revolt, however, was premature. Most men clung to wigs for a time, and the young hair rebels gave up the battle and returned to wigs themselves. Some young wig-wearers soon went to the other extreme, copying the overblown wig fashions promoted by a group of idle rich dandies who had made a grand tour of Italy together before returning to London to parade their male elegance. The "exquisite young fops" formed what they called The Macaroni Club, in opposition to the conservative Beefsteak Club. Macaronis and those who tried to ape them adopted everything that was the most extreme in male fashion. Their outraged elders began calling anything that was new and outlandish "Macaroni."

Plain hair, without wigs, threatened to come back to men's heads, and even to some faces. But the revolt in the 1760s was premature.

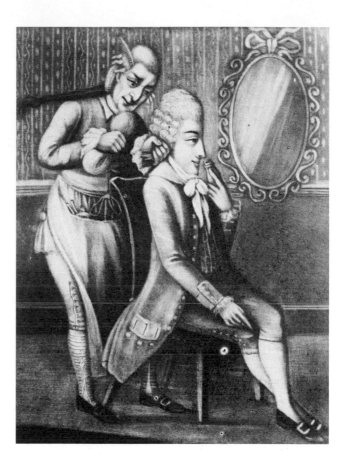

An 18th century caricature, not greatly exaggerated, making fun of the Macaroni's hair. The enormous broad queue at the back is being doubled into the "club" that will hang at the nape of his neck. *Prints Division, The New York Public Library, Astor, Lenox and Tilden Foundations*

For years the word "Macaroni" was a synonym for an overdressed young man, on both sides of the Atlantic, so that even America's Yankee Doodle, when he came riding to town on his pony, "stuck a feather in his hat and called himself a Macaroni." In London, a popular song, *The Macaroni,* had a verse that went:

> Five pounds of hair they wear behind,
>   The ladies to delight, Oh!
> Their senses give unto the wind,
>   To make themselves a fright, Oh!
> This fashion who does e're pursue,
>   I think a simple-tony;
> For he's a fool, say what you will,
>   Who is a Macaroni.

Balanced on the Macaroni's head was an enormously high wig, with false hair swept up over a towering wire frame that was cushioned with pads of wool. Hanging from the wig was an equally enormous broad and

63

The ultimate in Macaroni, from an English caricature of 1773. His enormous wig and queue were reduced by other wearers to a reasonably small Cadogan. *Prints Division, The New York Public Library, Astor, Lenox and Tilden Foundations*

64

This caricature shows the Macaroni's influence on women's hair and makes fun of the idea that without money there would be nothing about the wealthy young fop to interest a girl. *Prints Division, The New York Public Library, Astor, Lenox and Tilden Foundations*

flat queue, which was doubled up upon itself and tied around the middle so as to suspend it in a "club" just below the back of the neck.

The Macaroni fad influenced hair styles for women and even for children. In a much more moderate form, the Cadogan Wig, with a lower upswept foretop and a smaller clubbed pigtail, became extremely popular with men. But the Macaronis had taken wigs about as far as they could go, and a backlash against extreme foppery brought a new revolt. Once more, there were those who shucked their wigs, boldly bared their own hair, and even gave up powdering it.

In France, philosopher Jean Jacques Rousseau had complained bitterly, "The poor are without bread because we must have powder for our hair." He was echoed in England by a poetic warning that:

> Their hoarded grain, contractors spare,
> And starve the poor to beautify the hair.

Poor wheat harvests, scant supplies of flour for food, and high prices brought rioting. People looted bakers' shops for bread and tradesmen were dragged into court, accused of holding back flour to sell it for wig powder. But the wealthy went right on powdering wigs, and some even dusted the hair of their pet dogs with powder.

The end of the wig was hastened in France when the people of Paris rose to storm the Bastille on July 14, 1789, and began the Revolution against the royal establishment that had answered their cries for bread with, "Let them eat cake." The powdered wig and its dangling queue became a symbol of the hated aristocracy. As hundreds of aristocrats were trundled off to the guillotine, others decided to give up their wigs rather than lose their heads entirely. Freedom of hair became as much a mark of the French patriot as the Liberty Cap that covered it. Defiant Revolutionaries wore their hair deliberately disheveled, sometimes hanging in a disordered tangle to their shoulders, in contempt for the wig-wearers of the old regime. Others cut it short and ragged.

Hair battle between a French Democrat and an Aristocrat, drawn during the period of the French Revolution. The Aristocrat is trying to pull the Liberty Cap from the head of the Democrat, who has the Aristocrat's queue gripped in his fist as he tries to rip off his fancy wig.

Politics divided hair in England, too. Young liberals who sympathized with the Revolution in France wore theirs short, but the majority of men, loyal subjects of the king, remained wigged and powdered. Some conservative English Tories felt so strongly about it that they refused to send their sons to schools taught by men who went without wigs, branding such short-haired rebels as "dangerously radical."

Britain's poor raised an outcry for bread in the 1790s as flour prices soared again and the lack of wheat threatened famine. The London Privy Council and many English town governments called on people to quit powdering their wigs so that "a great quantity of wheat may be saved to the nation," and the mayor of Great Yarmouth counseled that "appearances are at all times to be sacrified to the public weal."

What such appeals failed to do, a tax finally accomplished. England's Prime Minister William Pitt, whose government was sorely in need of funds, had a law put through Parliament in 1795 to tax every citizen, male or female, who insisted on using hair powder, one guinea a head. The tax brought more than £200,000 into the treasury in its first year, and also gradually ended more than a century of wig-wearing.

Opponents of the tax, led by the Duke of Bedford, met at Woburn Abbey, according to the *London Times,* for "a general cropping and combing out of hair-powder." They were young nobles and gentlemen who already had given up wearing wigs, but who until then had still powdered their own long hair, which they wore braided in queues. In protest, they snipped off their pigtails, cropped their hair short, and signed a pact "to forfeit a sum of money if any wore hair tied or powdered" again.

All over England, "crop clubs" sprang up. Typical was one in Lambeth, where the *Times* reported "every member . . . is obliged to have his head docked as close as the Duke of Bridgewater's old bay coach horses." Men everywhere began discarding wigs and powder for short-cropped plain hair of their own. Those who kept their wigs, and paid one guinea for the privilege of powdering, were mocked as "guinea pigs." There were so many converts to natural hair that powder tax revenues slowly dwindled to nothing.

Women meanwhile had been going through a hair revolution of their own. At the start of the 18th century, they gave up their *fontanges* and wore their hair quite simply for a while, lowered and dressed more or less closely to the head. But some males were suspicious that women were just taking a deep breath before they sent their hair shooting up again.

Madame de Pompadour, mistress of France's Louis XV, started the new upward trend in mid-century by arranging her hair "in a hundred entrancing ways . . . till the court nearly went mad attempting to imitate her inimitable coiffures." She gave hair one of its enduring fashions, the style of dressing it without a part, combed straight back from the forehead and worn high at the front. But for the 18th century's women, that was just the foundation they built upon. Taking off from where the pompadour began, they padded, puffed, stuffed, and swept false hair up over wire frames until the towers of the previous generation were dwarfed by ranges of hair "that rivaled the Alps."

Artists mocked, writers ridiculed, and furious males wrote angry letters to the newspapers, but the hair-raising women made it evident there were still more fantastic heights for their hair to climb. Taking a cue from the Macaronis, the ladies soon outdid them. Hairdressers for women flourished, most of them men who apparently were dedicated to turning women's hair into upside-down wastebaskets stuffed with almost any trash that came to hand.

Bushels of cotton wool, shreds of rope, horsehair, bran or straw were used for stuffing, mounded upon felt pads or cap wigs, with the natural hair brought up over the wire frames and masses of false hair added. Then the whole thing was cemented with a paste that hardened, and the outer shell was greased and floured with powder, decorated with gauze, tulle, pearls and jewels. Creating a headdress was a problem in engineering that required a full day's time.

Once the structure was built it remained undisturbed for from two to nine weeks. Some women slept with their necks on wooden supports to preserve their artificial "heads." The top-heavy oval of trash, which made a woman up to three feet taller than she really was, also caused the rebuilding of some homes, to raise ceilings and widen doorways. Even so, women sometimes had to enter rooms on their knees, and

68

kneel on the floors of sedan chairs and carriages, or else change the carriages, too, so they were open-topped to accommodate their hair.

The *London Magazine* complained that the "present prodigious, unnatural, monstrous, and dirty mode of dressing the hair" made it "at once shine and stink upwards." A letter writer agreed that "attracted by my eyes to approach as near as I could to these beautiful creatures, I have soon been repelled by my nose and been obliged to retire at a respectful distance." Another critic of women's hair put his pungent objections in verse:

> When he scents the mingled steam
> Which your plaster'd heads are rich in,
> Lard and meal, and clouted cream,
> Can he love a walking kitchen?

Hair was not really *this* high, but caricaturists had fun picturing it this way. Note that the man on the ladder has a Macaroni wig on himself, while the one with the sextant has a long pigtail. Another humorous conception of the structural work required, supposedly a hair dressing academy in Paris in 1788, is shown on the title page.

70

Greasy hair stuffed with things liable to rot as they went untouched through hot summer months provided a lively business for perfumers. Almost every dressing table was equipped with a "scratcher," a long-handled stick with a hooked end for stabbing through the hair to give some relief from itching. But despite hazards, dirt, discomfort, mockery and rage, fashionable women kept their hair high.

"Be Not Amazed Dear Mother, It Is Indeed Your Daughter Anne" *Prints Division, The New York Public Library, Astor, Lenox and Tilden Foundations*

The Butcher's Wife *Prints Division, The New York Public Library, Astor, Lenox and Tilden Foundations*

Another French king's lady, Louis XVI's frivolous and arrogant Queen Marie-Antoinette, promoted the fashion of attaching ostrich plumes, some of them four feet high, to heads, and the ballrooms of London and Paris soon became "forests of waving feathers." She also amused herself by playing at farming at her summer palace and that started ladies hanging carrots, onions and other fresh vegetables on their hair. One day the queen hummed a tune from a favorite opera, and a few days later her ladies appeared with model stage settings for scenes from the opera on their heads.

When the French ship *La Belle Poule* won a victory over the English warship *Arethusa,* Frenchwomen celebrated the event by re-creating the battle on seas of hair, with model ships, fully rigged and manned with toy sailors. Others took to creating hair-dos that formed the back-drop for scenes from novels, plays, poems, happenings in the news,

The French Lady in London   *Prints Division, The New York Public Library, Astor, Lenox and Tilden Foundations*

73

events in history, fields of sheep and shepherds, models of the city of Paris, landscapes, mountains, windmills, waterfalls.

The craze spread to England and so shocked some men that they stopped criticizing each other's hair to turn their full fury against feminine head whims that represented small zoos with caged lions and tigers of blown glass, aviaries with miniature swans and peacocks, and such varied things as drowned chickens, mad dogs, cupids, nymphs, the solar system in movement, and balloon ascensions. One mourning widow had her husband's tombstone, in miniature, erected in her hair; another outdid her with a model hearse drawn by six white horses.

Various headdresses from books of the fashion of the times.

74

Marie-Antoinette suddenly switched directions, after losing most of her own hair during an illness, and helped lower hair again. The high constructed headdress was replaced with masses of curls that hung to the shoulders, or with frizzed and bushy hair that one writer of the time criticized as "absolutely a lion's mane."

The French Revolution eventually cost the queen not only her hair but her head, and the threat of the guillotine also subdued the hair styles of other aristocratic ladies, even those in England who were far removed from such an act of final criticism. It was not a time for the noble and wealthy to call attention to the extravagance of hair. Women, like men, ended the century with shorter, more natural hair.

But some Frenchwomen couldn't resist a final mocking hair salute to the guillotine itself, as if giving answer to those who had forced them to take down their hair. They shaved it to the nape of the neck, so it was shingled up the back, in imitation of the way heads of those condemned were shorn before execution. And to add a dramatic touch, they covered their cropped hair with shawls of blood red.

- III -

In early 18th century America, where beards and moustaches were rarely seen, the long black beard of the English pirate, Captain Edward Teach (or Thatch), symbolized his evil character to people of the coastal Carolinas and Virginia. Called "Blackbeard" because of it, the blood-thirsty buccaneer sailed his pirate ships out of the West Indies to rob, loot, and pillage whole towns of beardless men. Terrible tales were told of his beard, which he reportedly tied off in knots with squibs of gun-powder when he was about to raid some town and slaughter its people. Even his own men, it was said, ducked to hide under tables when the pirate lovingly caressed his beard, because that was a sure sign that he was in a murderous mood.

Some colonial American frontiersmen let their beards grow, but in settled communities nearly all men shaved regularly. There were no moustaches or beards on the faces of the signers of the Declaration of Independence. Even tolerant Benjamin Franklin described a man he knew as an eccentric because he wore a beard. When future Chief Justice John Marshall neglected shaving during a hike overland from Virginia to Philadelphia as a young man, keepers of rooming houses refused him a bed because of his "slovenly" bearded appearance. And a Philadelphia girl, Elizabeth Drinker, noted in a letter that she had seen an elephant and two bearded men on the streets of that city the same day. She

The black beard of pirate Edward Teach was a terror in clean-shaven Colonial America.

Advertisement, New York *Gazette,* May, 1750

THIS IS TO ACQUAINT THE PUBLIC THAT THERE is lately arrived from London the Wonder of the World, an *Honest* Barber and Peruke Maker, who might have worked for the King, if his Majesty would have employed him: It was not for the want of Money he came here, for he had enough of that at Home, nor for the want of Business, that he advertises himself. BUT to acquaint the Gentlemen and Ladies, *that Such a Person is now in Town,* living near *Rosemary Lane* where Gentlemen and Ladies may be supplied with Goods as follows, viz: Tyes, Full Bottoms, Majors, Spencers, Fox-Tails, Ramalies, Tacks, cut and bob Perukes: Also Ladies Tatematongues and Towers after the Manner that is now wore at Court. By their Humble and Obedient Servant,

JOHN STILL

obviously considered the beards as remarkable as the elephant.

It was an American age that dictated men were to have no hair of their own on their faces, but at the same time insisted they should have false hair on their heads. Europe's wigs came to America in every style by the thousands, so that by the mid-1700s there was hardly a town dweller of any class or calling who would shame himself by wearing his own hair in public.

Fashionable American boys were rigged out in wigs from the age of seven. College students had flat-topped bag wigs. Virginia gentlemen, Massachusetts magistrates, low-paid parsons, craftsmen, and apprentices wore them. Some house slaves were required to wear white goat's hair or horsehair wigs. Many wigs were American-made, but wealthy men imported theirs from England.

A man could outfit himself with hat, coat, shirt, breeches and shoes for about what a good wig cost. Dressing wigs and caring for them also was expensive. Most barbers were paid a yearly fee that included shaving the patron's face and head as well as dressing his wig.

American gentlemen kept their wig styles right up to date. When Englishmen shortened them, so did the colonials. Later in the century, they even imitated London's Macaroni dandies, with less extravagance but with hair looped up and pinned in place with a comb. Yankee Doodle wasn't the only wig-sporty American who hoped to be taken for a Macaroni.

But in country areas, especially in parts of the South where many settlers were poor and farms were far apart, men often ignored wigs and wore their own hair, usually covered with the sort of thin cap that city dwellers wore only at home or when going to bed. Some city visitors to such regions were shocked by the sight of men appearing in public without wigs.

When Thomas Jefferson was a young college student at William and Mary he went without any wig to cover his thick red hair. But when he became a member of the Virginia House of Burgesses he also became a regular customer of Williamsburg wigmaker Edward Charlton. Jefferson experimented with wigs, first buying a brown dress queue wig, then a brown tie wig, and finally settling for the brown dress bob that was the prevailing style. As ambassador to France in the 1780s he wore a formal powdered wig. Still later, he wore his own hair again, at first powdered and with a queue down the back, and then in a more natural manner, rather short but bushy.

When the Minute Men of Revolution rose from the countryside against the British their ranks included long-haired rebels without wigs.

Thomas Jefferson

Those who came out of the Virginia hills in the fall of 1775 to march on the capital at Williamsburg looked "so savage," with their long hair falling behind them, untied and unqueued, that bewigged townsmen boarded their doors against them.

New England patriots, although many were wigged themselves, showed contempt for elaborate wigs of the Tories by ripping some of them off their heads. Among Tories roughly handled in Boston was James Murray, who wrote that a crowd "made sport" of him by holding his arms and pulling off his wig. He was forced to parade home with his "pate . . . left exposed" while a jeering mob followed with his "wig dishevelled . . . borne on a staff behind."

The Revolution turned some men against wigs, but most were a long time in discarding them. The signers of the Declaration of Independence although clean-shaven, showed no Republican attitude in hair styles. Some were elaborately wigged and others dressed and powdered their hair in a way that hardly separated them from the wig-wearers. Wigs generally remained in fashion in the United States until European men began to give them up after the French Revolution.

80

American soldiers of the Revolution wore their hair as they pleased, often long and unbound, and many also went without shaving, until George Washington decided in 1780 that something should be done about neater appearance. He ordered that they were to "appear upon the Grand and other parades shaved, combed and powdered, and their Cloaths as clean as Circumstances will admit."

Two years later Washington suggested uniformity in hair styles. It would be "a very considerable ornament," he said, for soldiers "to wear the hair cut or tied in the same manner throughout a whole corps," and where conditions made that impossible he ordered that there should be at least "similarity in a company." So began the Army's hair regulations, which some soldiers were to grumble about forever after.

George Washington seldom, if ever, wore a wig. Although he lived in an age of wigs and was a fashion-conscious man, he preferred his own hair. He wore it as it grew, naturally brown and unpowdered, when he was a member of the Virginia House of Burgesses. During the Revolution he powdered it white and braided the back of it into a queue, which he tied with a ribbon or covered with black silk bag. He kept the queue and white powder in later years, but wore his hair lower on top and with the sides bushy.

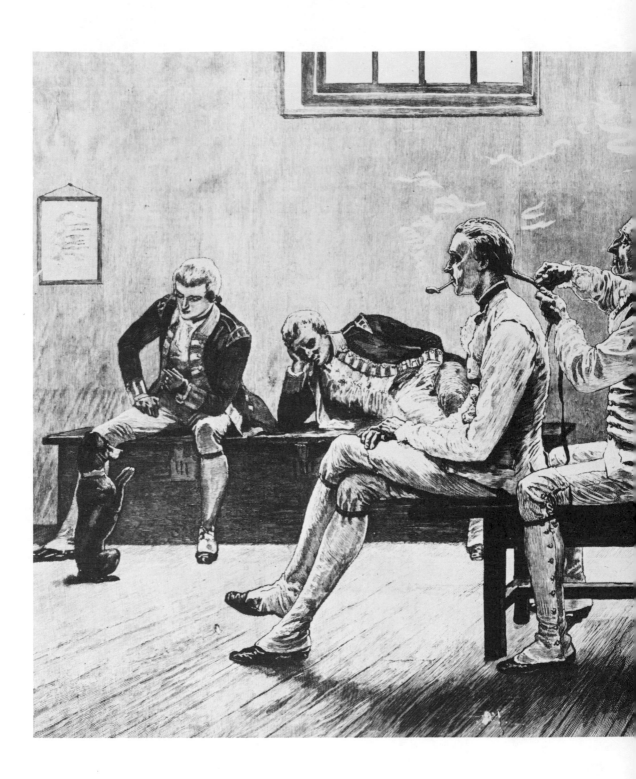

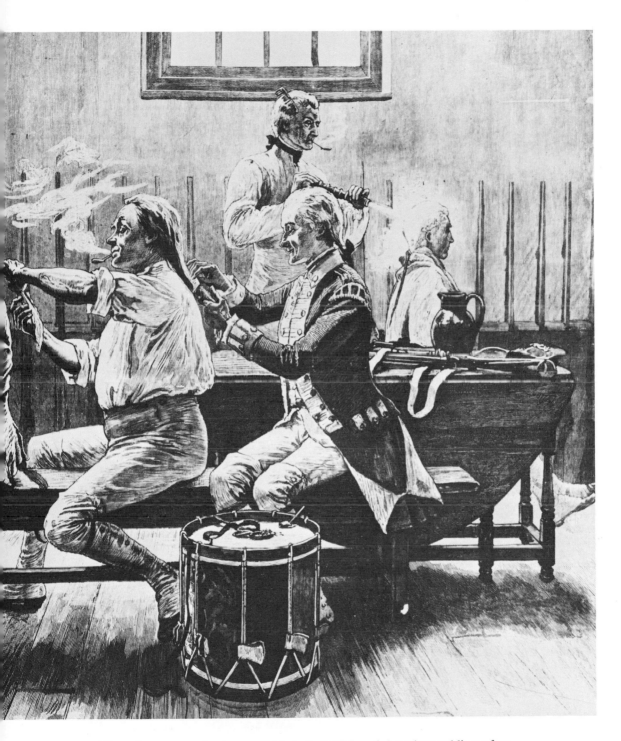

When there was no barber available both British and American soldiers often did their own hair. This old *Harper's Bazar* engraving, from a painting by Frank Dadd, shows men combing, braiding, and ribbon-binding each other's queues. The man at the right, wrapped in covering cloth, is having his hair powdered.

John Adams

John Adams was glad to give up his wig. He had to wear one, a heavily powdered and formal wig, when he was ambassador of the new United States in France and England. But by the time he came home and became Vice-President, going wigless was a growing Republican mode. Adams tested the matter during a summer away from Washington, by leaving his wig off while relaxing at his Quincy, Massachusetts, home. He looked so different some friends failed to recognize him, and there were critics who complained that without his wig the Vice-President had "hair like a farmer's."

Despite criticism, Adams enjoyed going without his itchy wig in warm weather. After that, he sometimes wore it and sometimes not, and finally gave it up entirely, but powdered his hair. Other men had discovered the same freedom and the long reign of wigs was all but over. As in Europe, some men were timid at first and wore their hair combed to imitate a wig. Others declared their full independence and cut it quite short.

America's colonial women lifted, twisted, tortured, and curled their hair to match every changing European style. Fashionable city girls came into the mid-18th century with powdered hair pinned up quite short in back, and with large curls at the front, which one critic said looked like "eggs on strings." But before long feminine hair-dos started an upward artificial climb that gradually would lift them over cushions, stuffings of wool, and wire frames. As early as 1766 an observer wrote, " 'Tis almost impossible to make the ladies understand that heads bigger than one's body are ugly."

Upward climb of women's hair. Socially prominent New Yorker at the time of the Revolution, Mrs. Catherine Duer.

A ten-year-old girl, Ann Winslow, visiting her aunts in Boston in 1770, told of being fitted with a new "Heddus roll" which one aunt said "ought to be made less" and another aunt said "ought not to be made at all." In a letter to her mother, Ann said the headdress was made of mixed cow tail and horsehair, with a little yellow hair "taken out of the back part of an old wig." With it on, her head was taller than her face was wide, but she wrote: "It makes my head itch and ach and burn like anything, mama."

As Revolution neared, the patriotic Daughters of Liberty pledged themselves to boycott British imports of false hair and appealed to others to give up such luxuries. When the thirteen colonies declared Independence in 1776 some American women paid tribute by wearing their hair in thirteen rolled curls. But even the war failed to stop the upward climb of hair fashion.

American males denounced girls in British-occupied cities for wearing their hair in ways to attract Redcoats and handsome young officers of His Majesty's forces. When Americans made an alliance with France, women's interest in keeping their hair up was influenced by the arrival of French soldiers, who must have been made to feel almost at home by the revival of Paris styles on the heads of American women. "The hair of the head is raised and supported upon cushions to an extravagant height," one Frenchman wrote from New England in 1781. What he found even more surprising was that "instead of powdering they often wash the head."

New England clergymen were less pleased. The Reverend Manasseh Cutler complained in 1781 that the wife of Washington's close adviser, General Henry Knox, had a hair-do that reminded him of "the monstrous devil." Her hair, he said, was "craped at least a foot high" in front, "much in the form of a churn bottom upward." But that same year the fashion news reaching America from Europe was that ladies were wearing "heads about 2 inches high and not very broad with 2 small Curles of a side." In the new United States towering feminine heads soon were lowered. Like America's men, its women had declared their independence, but when it came to hair Europe still dictated what would be worn.

Rebels against the establishment, both in Europe and America, cut their hair short at the start of the 19th century to set themselves apart from conservatives of the old order who still powdered their hair and wore it tied in queues. Wigs, although some were still worn, had gone out of fashion, but powdered queues were a lingering fashion.

Young men of France took their inspiration from the short haircuts of ancient Rome and had their hair clipped in back and brushed away in all directions from the crown of the head, so that it fell in a natural tangle over the forehead. As the new fashion spread through Europe and to America, men's hair in the United States became a political issue.

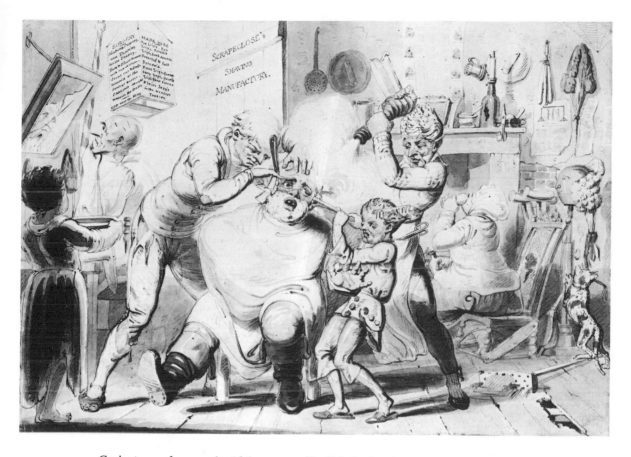

Caricature of an early 19th century English barbershop. *Prints Division, The New York Public Library, Astor, Lenox and Tilden Foundations*

Republican followers of Thomas Jefferson, new democrats who sympathized with the French radicals, were taunted by long-haired Federalists who mockingly shouted, "Frenchy! Frenchy!" To some Federalists the short-haired Jeffersonians looked like "frightened owls" or like men "fighting a hurricane backwards." Moralists warned that a wave of French "anarchy, radicalism and immorality" was invading America on men's heads and that their hair was an expression of the "alien political concepts" in their minds.

Most barbers in the muddy little new capital city of Washington

Young Americans with short "frightened owl" haircuts that enraged longhairs of the older generation.

seemed to side with the Federalists, if only because they feared a loss of business with the coming to power of the short-haired Jeffersonians. During Federalist days the barbershops clustered along Pennsylvania Avenue seldom had enough high-backed chairs to seat all the hairy politicians who came to gossip while they had their heads powdered and their queues carefully dressed. Washington's barbers complained that the new democrats, even when they didn't cut off most of their hair, wore it carelessly, in short little queues tied off with ribbon.

John Randolph, leader of the Republicans in congress, was described as "eccentric in the extreme" by a visiting Philadelphia girl, Phoebe Morris, who wrote home to her father that Randolph's "hair is long and simply confined by a ribbon, not in the style of a queue, but as you wear yours sometimes of a morning when you first get up."

But gradually, although reluctantly, even the Federalists began to shorten their hair. The world's military services also gave in to changing styles and first ordered a shortening and then a complete cutting off of queues. In the British Army, men were paraded out by regiments so each soldier could chop off his comrade's pigtail, and some entire regiments were shorn in ten minutes.

When the men who had started the 19th century by cutting their hair short became the older generation, younger men began to let their hair grow long. By mid-century it was mostly older men who continued to comb their hair forward, Roman style, as they had in their youth, often to conceal oncoming baldness. The new youth movement was for hair that hung bobbed, sometimes in ringlets produced with curling irons.

But that trend was hardly established before the rage was all for straight, smooth hair, parted at the side.

Young fops and dandies tried to imitate England's exquisite Beau Brummell, who reportedly employed three coiffeurs to fix his hair, one to do his front locks, a second his side locks, and a third specialist to care for the hair at the back of his head. But young liberals of the emerging Romantic movement had a different idol, the poet Lord Byron. His free life style and his writings influenced young men all over Europe and in America. Thousands took to wearing flowing "Byronic locks" in imitation of Byron's rather long and wavy chestnut hair. They also slicked their hair into place with the Macassar Oil that Byron mentioned in the lines of his poem *Don Juan:*

> In virtues nothing earthly could surpass her,
> Save thine 'incomparable oil', Macassar!

The hair oil whose sales he boosted supposedly came from nut kernels

John Randolph

89

Young men who changed hair lengths faced problems. "Our Fast Young Man has just dropped in to have 'a month's growth' taken off," according to this 1859 English caricature. "The result will entail a visit to his Hatter." *Prints Division, The New York Public Library, Astor, Lenox and Tilden Foundations*

of trees in the Celebes Islands, but most of it that flooded the market in Byron's time and for years afterwards was locally made of such things as cloves, mace, and oil of cinnamon. Despite its critics, Macassar Oil became so popular in America and the rest of the world that housewives began putting lace doilies on the backs of chairs and sofas to protect them from the grease men used to slick and shine their hair, and the little oblongs of cloth took the name *antimacassar,* which they still have today.

Young Don Juans who couldn't afford Macassar Oil larded their hair with tallow or bear's grease, which also helped some of them produce the popular "cow lick," a single curl over the forehead. Another popular male hair fad was to roll the hair at the front of the head in what was known as a Piccadilly Fringe. By mid-century writers were coming to the defense of long hair for men. It was all a matter of "individual taste,"

90

according to *The Habits of Good Society,* published in London in 1859, and there was "nothing unmanly in wearing long hair, although undoubtedly it is . . . a temptation to vanity."

Both the critics and defenders of long hair might well have saved their breath. Although the center part remained popular, the length began to grow shorter once more. With London setting the style, men's hair at last seemed to settle down to a fairly short length for the rest of the century.

Legend has it that when General George Custer decided to have his hair cut short in 1876 the Indians who heard about it predicted that his shorn locks marked him as a man about to die, which he soon did in the Last Stand at the Little Big Horn River, but nobody knows how many of the men who died with him also had adopted the prevailing style for closer haircuts.

For other men, short hair had become so accepted that an American etiquette manual of 1869, *Good Society,* advised readers that the only men who indulged in long hair were "painters and fiddlers."

Some wore it long and some cut it short. Barbershop at Richmond, Virginia, 1861. *Picture Collection, New York Public Library*

The hair on men's faces caused more trouble in the 19th century than the hair on their heads. It had been so long since men wore beards that those who first tried to revive them were looked upon as freaks. America's outstanding champion of the beard was Joseph Palmer. Few men in history have been persecuted as he was for courageously defending his beard as a symbol of individual freedom against rigid small-town conformity. "I'll tell you why I wear it," he would say, "if anyone can tell me why other men 365 days a year scrape their faces from nose to neck."

Palmer was a hard-working, God-fearing farmer, a descendant of early New England colonists. His grandfather had fought in the Revolution and he himself was a veteran of the War of 1812. He also was a philosopher of sorts, a crusader for many reforms, whose friends included Emerson, Hawthorne, and Thoreau. With Bronson Alcott, father of Louisa May Alcott, he later became one of the founding fathers of a short-lived New Eden, a farm commune at Fruitlands, whose members turned from worldly materialism to seek a quiet and unpretentious living from the land.

But when Palmer moved into Fitchburg, Massachusetts, as a butcher and farm produce merchant in the 1830s the townspeople denounced him as "un-American" and worse. He was called "a human monster" and a "fiend incarnate," despised, shunned, jeered at. Men avoided his company, women crossed the street rather than pass close to him, and mothers frightened unruly children with the warning that Palmer would "get them" unless they behaved.

In clean-shaven Fitchburg, Palmer was a social outcast solely because he dared to wear a long beard, which made him look different from other men, and that outraged the whole community. Even in metropolitan Boston, when he visited the big city to attend an anti-slavery conference, Palmer's beard attracted such a threatening street crowd that he finally had to be rescued by police. Hardly any man in New England then wore a beard and certainly no other man had worn such a beard in Fitchburg within living memory.

Palmer was hooted on the street, sometimes pelted with stones and clods of earth, and his son's boyhood was made miserable by schoolmates who taunted him because of his father's beard. Fitchburg's clergymen labored to convince Palmer that "to wear whiskers was worse than a disgrace; it was a sin." The town's rage boiled over one Sunday when Palmer, after being refused communion at church, created a scene. He had knelt with the rest of the parishoners at the communion rail, but the minister passed him by and pointedly ignored him. Palmer angrily strode to the communion table, took the cup into his own hands and

Joseph Palmer, who dared to be different, with the beard he defended against an entire New England community. *Fruitlands Museums, Prospect Hill, Harvard, Mass.*

lifted it to his lips, and then faced the shocked clergyman and congregation and told them, "I am a better Christian than any of you."

He was coming out of the Fitchburg Hotel one day not long after that when four men seized him and threw him to the stone steps, badly injuring his back. They were armed with scissors, determined to cut off his beard, but despite his pain Palmer managed to pull out a pocketknife and slash at them in self-defense. He saved his beard but stabbed the legs of two of his attackers, and was arrested on a charge of committing "an unprovoked assault."

Palmer argued in court that he was the one who had been assaulted, but a judge found him guilty and fined him. That seemed so unfair Palmer refused to pay the fine and was dragged off to the county jail, where he was imprisoned for more than a year. His jailers cursed him, spat upon him, encouraged fellow prisoners to threaten him. Five men entered his cell and made an attempt to pin him to his bunk and shave him, but Palmer beat up two of them and sent the others fleeing.

He was removed to a cellar dungeon, kept in solitary confinement, given little to eat or drink. Once when he begged for water, a jailer threw a bucket of it over him, and to satisfy his thirst Palmer had to sop up the drippings from the floor with scraps of bread. But with the help of his son, who tied a string to a rock and tossed it through the cell window, Palmer smuggled out letters to newspapers and high county officials, complaining about his mistreatment for the sole "crime" of wearing a beard.

Some people began to sympathize and there was such a public furor that officials finally came to his cell and asked him to forget the whole thing and to get out and go home. Palmer refused. "You put me in here," he told them, "and you'll have to put me out." They did just that. Hefting him into a chair, they carried him down the jailhouse stairs and deposited him on the walk outside.

He kept his beard for another forty years, made his farm a visiting place for famed philosophers, advanced thinkers, and reformers, and for any ordinary wayfarers who happened along to enjoy companionship at his fireside. Before he died at the age of eighty-four in 1875 most of the men who had condemned him were wearing beards themselves. His struggle was perpetuated in a stone monument at his grave, a cemetery bust of him with free-flowing whiskers. Beneath it, carved for eternity, were his name and the words: "Persecuted for wearing the beard."

"Persecuted for wearing the beard." Gravestone of Joseph Palmer, Evergreen Cemetery, Leominster, Mass. *Fruitlands Museums, Prospect Hill, Harvard, Mass.*

Beards began a comeback in France in the 1830s on the chins of young writers, artists, and political liberals. To those who claimed to represent Young France, beards were a common badge of revolt, an outward display of identifying themselves with whatever was new, daring, different.

"When a party of young Frenchmen approach one, it is like the advance of a herd of goats," the *New Monthly Magazine* told English readers in 1844. "Fortunately it is easier just now for England to pluck France by the beard than for France to return the affront. We are still respectable and razored."

France, personified by the Beard, and England by a clean-shaven Punch-like figure in an 1845 caricature.

Few Englishmen or Americans were bearded like the French, but hair was beginning to creep back to their faces, first as long side patches in front of the ears and as moustaches. In that same year of 1844, Charles Dickens, then a young man in his thirties, expressed his delight over a new set of lip whiskers. "The moustaches are glorious, glorious," he wrote a friend. "I have cut them shorter and trimmed them a little at the ends to improve their shape. They are charming, charming. Without them Life would be a blank."

Moustaches had first come back to glory on the upper lips of military men. German and French soldiers wore them, and then British artillerymen. Some young French civilians, not yet courageous enough to grow moustaches of their own, put on false moustaches to parade through the streets of Paris in a political demonstration in July, 1830. A month later young men in Brussels also staged a march, wearing fake moustaches as symbols of revolt.

German revolutionaries wore real ones, and in 1838 the King of Bavaria, considering moustaches signs of dangerous radicalism, forbade citizens to wear them under penalty of arrest. Meanwhile in Naples, university students caught wearing moustaches were dragged into barbershops by police, who stood by to enforce the use of the razor.

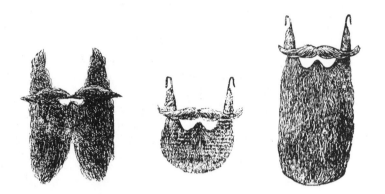

Young rebels donned fake beards and moustaches for street demonstrations.
Picture Collection, New York Public Library

Most male chins remained bare while side whiskers grew, sometimes worn with moustaches but more often worn alone. What began at the temples in the 1840s gradually bushed down the sides of men's faces, growing fuller and bushier for some twenty years but halting well above still naked chins. Side whiskers paved the way for the return of beards but it was a long time before they completed the circle.

Some American military officers wore hair at the sides of their faces in the War of 1812 and some civilians adopted the style. When Cadet Ambrose E. Burnside entered West Point in the 1840s he had the start of side whiskers that were to flourish in his later years as a general, setting a fashion for what became known as "burnsides." Twisted around, that became "sideburns." The French first dubbed them "side cutlets" because their shape resembled such cuts of meat, and the English translated that into "mutton chop whiskers."

English side whiskers waxed and waned according to words of approval or disapproval from royalty as well as to the dictates of fashion. But despite the scorn they sometimes aroused they generally kept length-

96

Londoners showing off their whiskers in Hyde Park. *Picture Collection, New York Public Library*

ening. Extra long bushes at the sides of the face were known as Piccadilly Weepers. They reached their extremes as Dundrearies, named for those worn by the character of Lord Dundreary in English dramatist Tom Taylor's popular play of the 1850s, *Our American Cousin*.

The role of Lord Dundreary was created for the New York production of the play by actor Edward Askew Sothern, whom it made famous. His repeated appearances in America and in England made him a stage idol and started a craze on both sides of the Atlantic for the enormous drooping whiskers that gave wearers what was described as the "baleful expression of a sad-eyed carriage dog."

When Napoleon's nephew proclaimed himself Emperor Napoleon III in 1852, after having overthrown the Republic to become a dictator of France, his long waxed moustache with the twirled ends and the little tuft of a goatee on his chin were quickly copied by his supporters, but French Republicans showed their opposition by wearing square-cut beards.

The beard style Napoleon III introduced became popular as an Imperial in other lands after beards were more common. It was worn, along with the traditional Van Dyke, by many American doctors, lawyers and professors, as well as by medicine show quacks, peddlers of patent nostrums, promoters of correspondence courses, and others who hoped it would give them a look of impressive authority.

Beards and moustaches were still stared at on the streets of English and American cities and to wear one took more than the mere courage to stand up to public contempt. In the professions, and in business generally, men who wore them often were judged unreliable. Young women were warned to think twice before marrying a man who went without shaving regularly because hairy faces were taken as an indication of "doubtful character."

Beard-wearing politicians were told their whiskers might cost them elections and some town governments fired minor officials who let their beards grow. The British House of Commons was shocked when

E. A. Sothern as Lord Dundreary.

Napoleon III and his moustache and beard Imperial.

one of its members, George Muntz, first appeared with a huge black beard and moustache, which seemed to arouse conservatives more than his radical political views. In 1850 a London barrister was driven from practice in Criminal Court after leaders of the bar moved to censure him for bringing ridicule on the legal profession because of his beard and moustache.

A Good Pennyworth.   *Prints Division, The New York Public Library, Astor, Lenox and Tilden Foundations*

Firms refused to hire bearded shopmen and salesmen. Businesses that ranged in kind from financial houses to lumberyards warned employees that beards or moustaches meant the loss of their jobs. Bearded male teachers were threatened with dismissal. London dock workers beat other workers who "put on airs" by growing moustaches. Hairy faces caused fist fights, public disturbances, and arrests. Among the many institutions that took a firm stand against lip whiskers was the Bank of England, which carefully avoided any suggestion of interference with what clerks did on their own time but issued an order that they were not to wear moustaches "during business hours."

Despite everything, beards and moustaches grew, and the controversy over them flamed into a war of words in the public press. Among beard defenders was the London writer of an 1847 book with a title as long as the beards themselves: *Beard Shaving and the Common Use of the Razor; an Unnatural, Irrational, Unmanly, Ungodly and Fatal Fashion among Christians.*

English caricature of 1854, showing a man with a birdcage over his head to protect his face from flying embers while he tries to force the growth of his moustaches by exposing them to the heat of the fireplace.

Taking a hint from the fair sex, this bearded male in a caricature by John Leech has put his beard in a hairnet.

But in 1850 a New York magazine, the *Knickerbocker,* took to the attack against beards with a series of articles that ran for three months. It was "an enormity no longer to be endured in silence," according to the *Knickerbocker*'s writer, John Waters, when "our yard-wide men, who in their youth have never imagined a beard at full-length except upon a maniac," appeared wearing beards themselves in "this community of sober merchants" to the "disgust of those of a more refined class." Declaring beards should be abolished "upon every principle of comity and social order," he held that "there exists no right whatever to exhibit to the community . . . a disgusting object of this sort."

Women joined in the argument by writing protests against having "our husbands, our brothers, our sons . . . wear nasty beards and look like Frenchmen." Some medical men answered by seriously advocating beards as protection against colds, sore throats, bronchitis, and the mumps. Outdoorsmen praised whiskers as nature's shield against rough weather, warming the face in winter and saving it from hot summer sun. "Man is born to work out of doors," Charles Dickens wrote in *Household Words* in 1853, while "woman was created for duties of another kind."

Perhaps the most influential promoter of beards was Alexander

Rowland, head of an English firm that manufactured products for the hair. His widely read book, *The Human Hair,* published in 1853, packed information and argument behind a vigorous plea for revival of the beard, and helped bring the full revolt that had been growing for a quarter of a century.

"Deprive the lion of his mane, the cock of his comb, the peacock of the emerald plumage of his tail, the ram and deer of their horns, and they not only become displeasing to the eye, but lose much of their power and vigor," Rowland wrote. "The caprice of fashion alone forces the Englishman to shave off those appendages which give the male countenance that true masculine character indicative of energy, bold daring, and decision."

Arguments for and against beards bombarded the public. Some beard-wearers took newspaper advertisements in self-defense and to encourage others to join them. The battle generated so much heat that a play by Robert Brough, *The Moustache Movement,* was a hit show in London. In it, a character questioned whether a girl loved him for himself, for he feared "it is the moustaches and not the man you love."

There were those who carried the fight to the grave. An upholsterer named Fleming wrote a will leaving a bequest to each of his employees, but specified that only half the amount was to go to any who were wearing moustaches at the time of his death. When Henry Budd died in 1862 he left half his estate to one son and half to another, with a provision that if either son grew a moustache the other son was to get the whole estate.

Soon there were so many beards the question for most men was not whether to wear one but what style to wear. Even etiquette manuals began to give approval. *The Habits of Good Society, a Handbook of Etiquette for Ladies and Gentlemen* said in 1859 that "the moustache and beard movement is one in the right direction, proving that men are beginning to appreciate beauty."

Evolution of Uncle Sam's Beard

OPPOSITE PAGE   Uncle Sam, like most Americans, stayed clean-shaven until around the time of the Civil War. Brother Jonathan was the name cartoonists first used to personify an unwhiskered United States, a mere lad among nations. Some early drawings showed him dressed like Benjamin Franklin and then he became a farmer who resembled Millard Fillmore. Almost always, Uncle Sam's hair was long and ragged. Traditionally he kept his beard after most American men again shaved off theirs.

Beardless Brother Jonathan, 1851.

Ten years later,
still without a beard.

Uncle Sam sprouts a small beard.

It grows longer.

Caricaturist Thomas Nast
brings Uncle Sam's beard
and hair to full growth.

An even more hairy Uncle Sam
during Spanish-American War.

The beard that came to stay.

Horace Greeley

BOTTOM   In 1852 when a beard, even on a man's chin, was a curiosity, showman P. T. Barnum drew crowds to his New York Museum by presenting the Bearded Lady of Switzerland.

104

New York newspaper editor Horace Greeley, whose advice to those seeking opportunity was, "Go West, young man," popularized the chin-saucer type of beard, copied by many admirers, who dubbed the style a *Greeley.* His chin-ringing whiskers provided political cartoonists with a nest of humor. As the London correspondent of his *New York Tribune,* Greeley hired another full-bearded man, Karl Marx.

Beards flourished in the West long before they were common in Eastern cities. Frontiersmen and the pioneers who pushed West by wagon, riverboat and rail seemed to leave their razors behind them. The rush of Forty-Niners seeking the wealth of the mines flooded California diggings and other rough camp towns with a sudden population that was mostly male. Shaving generally was ignored by the men who had few ladies about to curb their hairy ways.

The real American beard-rush began just before the Civil War. It had been coming for years, but the change seemed sudden and dramatic. As war began to divide men politically there was a national unity in whiskers. North and South, East and West, and for no clear reason, nearly all American men, middle-aged and older as well as young, started to grow facial hair and went on growing it for a generation.

A *Harper's Weekly* cartoon of the 1860s showing a little girl so puzzled by the strange growth of hair on her uncle's face that she doesn't know where to kiss him.

105

Sweeping moustaches linked sideburns and mutton chops. Grocery clerks and laborers, bankers, industrialists and railroad builders, sprouted box beards, spade beards, forked and twisted beards, goatees, Imperials and Greeleys. The chins of politicians soon were as bushed as those of the patriarchs of old. It was the age of the beard triumphant.

Beards became not only respectable but an evidence of reliability, even a trademark for cough drops. Newspapers and magazines were filled with advertisements for beard-growing preparations, promising thick whiskers in weeks, and etiquette books were revised to set new rules of conduct. "Never allow butter, soup or other food to remain on your whiskers," *Hill's Social Manual* advised. "Use the napkin frequently."

Clean-shaven President Franklin Pierce in 1853 had presided over a cabinet that included not a single man with a beard. Four years later, James Buchanan, called "the last of the doughfaces," had only one beard in his cabinet, that of Postmaster General Aaron Brown. Abraham Lincoln campaigned without a beard, but after his election he became the first President to wear one.

Lincoln had lived without whiskers for the first fifty-two years of his life when he decided, the January before his 1861 inauguration, to let them grow. During the campaign an eleven-year-old girl who had seen his picture wrote to tell him she thought he would look better with whiskers, but Lincoln had answered the childish fan letter by saying "as I have never worn any, do you not think people would call it a piece of silly affectation were I to begin wearing them now?"

Lincoln never explained to close associates, but something changed his mind and he had the beard by the time he left Illinois for Washington. When his train went through upstate New York, he remembered Grace Bedell, the little girl who had written to him, and arranged to have her meet him during a stop at Westfield where she lived. Lincoln stepped down to the platform to take her hand, give her a kiss, and tell her, "You see, I have let these whiskers grow for you, Grace."

Not all who attended Lincoln's inauguration approved the new beard. One critic, according to Lincoln's friend and biographer William Herndon, called the whiskers "of the blacking-brush variety, coarse, stiff and ungraceful," and said that they "spoiled, or at least seriously impaired, a face which, though never handsome, had in its original state a peculiar power and pathos." Among many cartoons about them was one in *Vanity Fair,* picturing an agent for a beard-growing ointment called "Lincoln Whiskeropherous," who was telling a customer, "Try one of them pots, and in three weeks you'll be as 'airy and as 'ansom as 'im."

WHISKERS IN THE
WHITE HOUSE

The haves and have-nots.

Buchanan

Lincoln

Johnson

Grant

Hayes

Garfield

Arthur

Cleveland

But the President's beard gave to beardless men whatever courage they still needed to grow beards of their own. In his cabinet, there were other notable beards, and the American male without a beard soon was the one people stared at as a curiosity. Andrew Johnson, who followed Lincoln into the White House, was a beardless exception among succeeding Presidents. Ulysses S. Grant was not only neatly bearded himself but had one of the hairiest cabinets in history.

Rutherford B. Hayes set a Presidential record with the length of his, and James Garfield maintained the bearded tradition in more limited fashion. Chester A. Arthur slipped back to side whiskers and moustache, but of a kind almost as bushy as a beard.

Grover Cleveland broke the spell. He came to the Presidency in 1885 with his chin and cheeks clean-shaven, beardless but with a moustache. Benjamin Harrison, the last of the whiskered Presidents, put the bare-chinned Cleveland out of the White House temporarily, but after four years Cleveland brought back the moustache for a second term.

Moustache cups, with built-in lip guards, were common when New York inventor Eli Randolph patented a moustache clip in 1872 to protect the moustache from the contents of any ordinary cup. It could be clipped to the nostrils as easily as a pair of glasses could be clipped to the bridge of the nose for what the *Scientific American* described as the purpose of "keeping one's moustache out of one's mush and milk."

After some thirty years of glory, American beards began to vanish once more, except on the faces of older men. Young men in England as well as America were turning against the beard. The new younger generation spared only their moustaches from the razor, as Grover Cleveland had. With chins cleared of beards, moustaches alone became the new symbol of youth in the Gilded Age. Before long, older men, chasing the image of youth, also were wearing their moustaches without "old-fashioned" beards.

President William McKinley appeared without even a moustache, has face entirely naked, to herald what a coming century would bring. But Theodore Roosevelt and William Howard Taft had moustaches, and held back the total shave for a while.

Women started the 19th century with their hair cut short, but soon seemed sorry and decided to let it grow long again. While nature was accomplishing that, they wore wigs, false braids and bunches of fake curls attached to combs that they could stick into place almost any-

A Fashionable Lady in Dress and Undress.   *Prints Division, The New York Public Library, Astor, Lenox and Tilden Foundations*

where. Some, for a time, favored a half-and-half hair-do which gave them a lopsided look, with one side of the hair flat and combed straight and the other side in clusters of curls. In other styles, braids became intricate, and instructions for braiding the hair sometimes were as complicated as those for knitting or crocheting.

Young women copied the hair whims of popular actresses and society beauties, and no one fashion lasted for long. They borrowed Macassar Oil from men to make their hair sleek and shiny. They brought it down over their cheeks, then tired of that and swept it up into big topknots, and soon tumbled it down again in ringlets and waterfalls of curls. The topknots moved to the backs of heads to become huge chignons.

But whatever they did, women kept adding false hair to their own. They spread it up over padded cushions, outward in twists and braids, downward in tons of curls, all of which needed false hair to eke out what nature provided. Professional hairdressers encouraged styles that required it and for a time women's own hair was almost lost in masses of artificial locks.

However women wore it, men found reason to criticize. Hardly a letter column in the newspapers was without some masculine appeal to women to give up all the false tumblings and curlings of hair. What particularly annoyed some men was the female habit of going about the house wearing hair curlers. "To see grapes in paper bags is bad enough," one complainant wrote, but to have "the rich locks of a lady in paper, the roots of the hair twisted up and the forehead staring bald . . . is a capital offence—a defiance of the love and admiration of the other sex."

Supplying women with false locks made from hair sheared from the heads of European peasant girls became a major industry. Tons of it were sold in London, Paris, and other cities, and the United States alone imported nearly 200,000 pounds of human hair, valued at close to a million dollars, in 1860. Within six years the amount had tripled and continued to increase steadily. Most of it came from rural areas of France and Germany where hair merchants dealt with it as they would with any annual farm crop brought to market.

Each spring agents made regular rounds of country districts to collect the hair poor farm girls had grown during the winter. Districts where girls drank a lot of beer and cider were considered especially rich for harvest, since it was said that those beverages increased the crop. Frances Trollope, telling about such a harvest in *Summer in Brittany,* wrote: "We saw several girls sheared, one after the other, like sheep,

110

and as many more standing ready for the shears . . . with their long hair combed out and hanging down to their waists." At each shearer's side was a large basket "into which every successive crop of hair, tied up into a wisp by itself, was thrown."

For their hair, the peasants got a few small coins, a trinket of cheap jewelry, or a gaudy cotton handkerchief. The collectors took it to the cities where merchants cleaned, sorted, graded, and curled it. By the time it reached the United States to be made into false hair pieces, the

The Human Hair Market at Alsace as pictured in 1871. Old woman seated at left is being offered scarf in trade for her wanted gray hair. At right, farm girl is being shorn. Behind her, girl at window is having her hair appraised by hair collector's agent.

111

hair was worth from $15 upwards a pound, depending on color, quality and length.

Behind the demand for such quantities of false hair were the big chignons women of fashion wore, at first low and at the backs of their heads, but then moved upward to spread the need in all directions. By 1863 *Godey's Lady's Book* was complaining that "perfect scaffoldings of hair are now built upon the head—roll upon roll—puff upon puff."

Calling some of the styles "extremely odd," the magazine described one which required the use of "two rats, two mice, a cat, and a cataract." Lest some reader might fear women were wearing dead rodents and pussy cats, *Godey's* hastened to explain that the terms referred to cushions of hair: "The rats are long frizetts of curled hair for the side rolls; the mice are the smaller ones above them; the cat is for the roll laid over the top of the head; and the cataract is for the chignon at the back of the head, which is sometimes called a waterfall, or *jet d'eau*."

A *Harper's Weekly* caricature of 1864 ridiculing hair-dos shown in fashion magazines of the time by suggesting these as "new styles of coiffure." Proposed were a dustmop, a nest of serpents, a "hare" for the hair, and at far right, *The Excelsior.   Picture Collection, New York Public Library*

Some critics denounced the pile-ups of false hair as "inhumane," calling attention to the plight of peasant girls who sacrificed their hair to the vanity of other women. Even angrier were those who protested that the style was plain ugly.

"This tumor-like excrescence disfigures the top of the head with the appearance of a horrid growth of disease which would seem to call for the knife of a surgeon did not we know that it could be placed or

Pictured in a Boston magazine for the inspiration of American girls in 1870 were these latest false hair fashions from England. But in England some men thought there should be a law against them. *Picture Collection, New York Public Library*

113

displaced at the will of the wearer," the *Bazar Book of Decorum* said, warning that such false hair came not only from the heads of peasants but also from "the dead of hospitals and prisons."

England's *Punch* magazine satirically suggested that Parliament should pass an act "for the abolition of chignons," under which it would be illegal "for any Female, whether single or married, to obtain or to become possessed by any means . . . of any Artificial Nobulous, hairy superfluity, or rotundive protuberance . . . or to dock and bedizen themselves in the style, fashion and eccentric mode generally adopted by ferocious and benighted cannibals." *Punch* also suggested that women be required to deposit their chignons at the nearest police station where they could be collected for use "as artificial Bird Nests for Intelligent Sparrows."

What American women wanted at the start of the 20th century was long hair. Those who lacked it sought the bottled magic of a thousand different products that promised to make it grow. Having "the longest hair in the world" made seven farm girls from upstate New York the envy of women everywhere as the 20th century began. Long hair became their career and earned them a fortune. "Seven Sutherland Sisters' Hair Grower and Scalp Cleaner always have been, are today, and will continue to be, perfect preparations for the production and maintenance of beautiful, soft, lustrous hair," they advertised. "Being sold by over 28,000 dealers should be evidence . . ." But the Seven Sutherland Sisters offered their own evidence, floor-length tresses that among the seven of them totaled a staggering thirty-six feet, ten inches in length.

Their father, Fletcher Sutherland, a poor Niagara County farmer and part-time lawyer and preacher, finding himself blessed with seven daughters who had the thickest hair anybody in those parts had ever seen, got up the "hair grower" that some folks said was mostly a mixture of rainwater and alcohol, and began exhibiting the girls, first at church socials and then in store windows. By the time he died, their fame was growing, and the Sutherland Sisters soon were stars of an act in the Barnum and Bailey Circus, where they thrilled spectators by standing in the spotlight to let their hair cascade down their backs.

The seven sisters went on to greater glory on personal tours, accompanied by seven maids to comb out their locks, and with the profits of their hair grower they built a mansion with marble bathrooms and swathed themselves in furs and jewels. Everything they did was news and for years their hair made Sutherland a household name. They also spent their money freely and when the last of the sisters died, in 1946, there was little of it left. But while they were at the height of their fame most

114

A woman's "Crowning Glory"

The century's first pin-up—
the Gibson Girl

women agreed with their advertising that popularized the slogan: "A woman's Crowning Glory is her hair."

The imaginary Gibson Girl was the ideal not only of women but of men, who made her the century's first pin-up. Created by Charles Dana Gibson, whose pen and ink drawings of her first appeared in *Life*, then a weekly humor magazine, she represented the "liberated young woman"

115

who swept up her hair and enjoyed the new freedoms of outdoor sports and indoor flirtation as she frankly charmed adoring males. Men dreamed of meeting a real-life girl who would match the Gibson Girl whose picture they pinned to their walls. And women tried their best to imitate her. They swept their hair up into a soft pompadour, puffed for a cloud effect, rolled from temple to temple over a horsehair "rat" to give it the width that went well with the Gibson Girl's tiny waist.

The men in Gibson's drawings, those who won her attention, summer or winter, were always clean-cut. Whatever their age, their hair was short and neatly trimmed, and to a man they were beardless, although they sometimes sported moustaches. American males, wishing themselves in such ideal feminine company, were influenced by the Gibson Girl to wear their own hair short and to shave their chins. For more than half a century, with minor variations, men kept the look the Gibson Girl helped inspire.

Summer and winter
—both sides of it.

117

Hailing the fact that the masculine world was beginning to shave again, *Harper's Weekly* advanced sanitary reasons "for reforming the beard," which "is, to be sure, very dirty . . . and is absurd besides." In the young, *Harper's* said, "it is grown purely for vanity" and "in age it forms the penalty of this vanity." By 1906 the *North American Review* was wondering whether the beard and moustache would ever again become popular because "after all, women make the fashion for men as well as for themselves, and the ticklishness inseparable from a growth of wiry hair in the vicinity of the lips . . . has become in their view obnoxious."

In France a group of men decided to conduct a scientific test of the danger of beards to young ladies who were kissed. One man who was bearded and one who was not bearded were walked through the crowded streets, stores, and museums of Paris, and were then brought back to a laboratory where each kissed a girl, in the interests of science. After each kiss, a sterilized brush was passed over the girl's lips, and was dipped in a sterile solution which was sealed and left standing for four days. Proof was offered that the lips of the shaven man carried only harmless germs, but that the kiss of the bearded man "literally swarmed with malignant microbes."

King Camp Gillette quickened the coming of the clean-shaven look with his safety razor. Gillette, a Fond du Lac, Wisconsin, salesman, had been searching for a product of some kind which customers would use once and throw away. While shaving himself with an old-fashioned cut-throat razor in 1895, he got the idea for a disposable razor blade, and was so inspired that he "stood before the mirror in a trance of joy."

By 1903 only 51 razors and 168 blades had been sold. But the next year the sales totals were ninety thousand razors and more than twelve million blades, and the amazing shaving revolution was underway. Barbers, still using old-fashioned razors and strops, grumbled that they were about to be put out of business by the "fad" of men shaving at home, but the barbershop survived, and so did some moustaches for a time.

The bristling moustache of Germany's Kaiser Wilhelm was widely copied by men who trained its growth with silk gauze binders strapped on at night to keep their lip whiskers pointing upward. But after Prussian militarism became unpopular, American barbers did a brisk business stubbing the flowering moustaches to toothbrush size. Thousands of upper lips sprouted with the sort of moustaches Charlie Chaplin soon would turn into a comic prop.

As the clean-cut look became the rule, men everywhere agreed that

King Camp Gillette, inventor of the safety razor with disposable blade, which started a shaving revolution. *The Gillette Company*

hair should be short and neatly trimmed, but there was some angry debate over how it should be parted. Men who parted their hair in the center were looked upon with suspicion by those who considered such non-conformity effeminate. By the same token, women who parted their hair on the side were denounced as "mannish." Gradually the center-part for men was accepted in most of the United States, along with the more usual side-parting, but there were pockets of resistance. The *Barbers' Journal* reported in 1904: "No man who parts his hair in the middle can ever carry Texas for the Presidency."

Men became the Pied Pipers of a crusade to drive the "rats" and false puffs out of women's hair. In magazine articles and letters to newspapers, they complained against extravagant feminine hair-dos that were built with pads and wire frames into spreading pompadours. One husband, quoted by the *Ladies' Home Journal* in 1911, told how his respect for his wife had fallen after he discovered her wearing "shams" in her hair. "The step from the wearing of a lie to the acting of a lie is not a long one," he moralized, warning that "many women fail to see that in the wearing of shams they are living a lie not only to themselves but to those nearest and dearest to them."

Women, bored with the pompadour and possibly tired of trying to compete with the Gibson Girl, eagerly joined in the revolt for more simplicity in hair styles and "rats" soon were on their way out. They first substituted height for width, by moving the bulk of their hair to

No More Hair Rats
THE COLVER PUFF POMPADOUR COMB

the back, but gradually shaped it more to the head. The pompadour began to disappear, helped by the Marcel wave, which imitated the natural curl of the hair by a curling iron process that kept its shape for several weeks.

Invented some years before by French hairdresser Marcel Grateau, who began his career as a stablehand currying the tails of horses, the Marcel wave revolutionized 20th century woman's hairstyling. Grateau had earned a fortune from it and had retired before its popularity really began to spread from Paris to the average woman in the rest of the world just before World War I. In mass production Marcel waves soon looked anything but natural, but they remained a standard beauty shop method into the 1930s.

Meanwhile a Swiss-born London hairdresser, Charles Nessler, had invented the first permanent waving system, which was to cause an even greater hair revolution. In 1906, when he first offered to put a permanent curl into women's hair by winding it spirally with the use of borax pads and a gas heater, only seventy-four women offered up their heads for the six-hour treatment. Within the next six years the annual total of permanents grew to five thousand. But it wasn't until after the First World War that most American women overcame their fears of shocks from electrified waving machines and accepted the permanent wave as a "necessity."

War had made long hair both a nuisance to women and a symbolic hindrance to freedom. Forced out of their homes and into factories, offices, and more active lives by the war, most women had little time to fuss with hair. They just wanted to get it out of the way, sometimes by winding it close to their heads, ear-muff fashion, and sometimes by cutting it short at the sides and restraining it with wrap-around cloth bandeaus. The more daring among them simply cut it short, and became the forerunners of a bobbed-haired generation.

Irene Castle, who first danced to fame in Paris and then in New York just before the First World War, with her aviator husband and partner, Vernon, helped set not only the tempo of the 1920s but also its hair. All of society copied the ballroom dances they originated, the one-step, hesitation waltz, turkey trot and Castle walk, and Irene introduced to the world of fashion the slim boyish figure and bobbed hair.

The bob was one of the oldest of hair fashions, worn by men and some women before Roman times, again during the Middle Ages, and was basically the common bowl-on-the-head haircut of the 1800s. But it had been more than a century since fashionable women cut their hair

120

Irene and Vernon Castle. The hair-do that started bobbed hair. Dancer Irene Castle, shown with her husband and partner Vernon, pace-setter for the international smart set of the World War I era, had her hair cut short, and doomed long tresses. With hairpins discarded, the headband was considered *chic* to hold the new bob in place. *United Press International, Inc.*

short, just after the French Revolution. The fad started again in Paris in 1912 with models and dancers who wore their hair Dutch Boy style. Popularized by Irene Castle, bobbed hair became an international rage and the century's most enduring fashion. For fifty years, in one style or another, women's hair would remain mostly short.

But in the early 1920s few national issues aroused America more than bobbed hair. Each woman had to face the crucial decision, to bob or not to bob, wondering whether the fashion would last. Tears and smelling salts accompanied the sacrifice as shorn cascades of crowning glory tumbled to the carpets of swank hairdressing salons and to the plain linoleum floors of barbershops. By May, 1922, the *American Hairdresser* was cautiously predicting that the bobbed hair craze "will probably last through the summer anyway . . ."

Women's hairdressers, alarmed by the number of women who were rushing into men's barbershops for boyish bobs that rounded their hair only a little longer than a man's haircut, made a determined effort to revive long hair in 1923, but failed. While men raged over the feminine invasion of the barbershop, women all but crowded them out. In some cities the clamor had long lines of women outside shops while others sat on the floors inside waiting their turn in the chairs.

New York alone soon reported heads being clipped at the rate of two thousand a day. Barber schools advertised quick courses that would teach the "Boy Bob" to any man's barber, and hairdressers countered by warning against the "free and easy" surroundings of male barbershops that were "unsuitable to the high standards of American womanhood."

To conservatives, short-haired women were as much "radicals and freaks of society" as long-haired musicians, artists, and anarchists. Some saw in bobbed hair a symbol of all the ills of the age, ranging from jazz, short skirts, sexy movies, the automobile, and prohibition to such threats as "Freudian psychology" and the "growing cult of the so-called free woman." The boyish bob, followed by the shingle and bingle which shaved the nape of the neck, and then by the curly bob and spit curls, were all part of what the older generation denounced as "Flaming Youth."

Preachers took to pulpits to warn that "a bobbed woman is a disgraced woman." In a Missouri courtroom, a mother pleading for the return of her six children who had been living with a guardian heard the oldest of them testify to the judge: "We don't believe mother is a Christian woman. She bobs her hair." Men divorced their wives over bobbed hair. Other males banded together with vows to give up shaving until wives agreed to let their hair grow out again. A large department store fired all bobbed haired employees and a hospital discharged bobbed haired nurses.

Some medical men argued in print that bobbing would result "in the ultimate baldness of the species," while others held that it would increase the growth of hair. Without bobbed hair no woman could hope to be really *chic,* stylists advised, but others insisted short hair robbed women of true femininity. *The Saturday Evening Post* commented in 1925 that "there hasn't been a newspaper published for the past two years . . . that hasn't carried some sort of a story about women's hair."

Mary Pickford, whose clusters of long drop curls had been idolized by women until bobbing began again, discussed her own dilemma. Her fans would be distressed and shocked, she feared, if she cut her hair short, but she admitted the day might come when "casting all caution to

Bobbed hair, to the alarm of men, led some women to have their hair cut short in men's barbershops, and some men called it a female invasion of "man's last stronghold." *United Press International, Inc.*

the winds, forgetting fans and family, I shall flee to a coiffeur and come out a shorn lamb to join the great army of the bobbed." And eventually, she did.

Opera star Mary Garden, who bobbed her hair in 1927 at the age of fifty, told readers of the *Pictorial Review:* "Bobbed hair is a state of mind and not merely a new manner of dressing my head. . . . I consider getting rid of our long hair one of the many little shackles that women have cast aside in their passage to freedom. Whatever helps their emancipation, however small it may seem, it is worthwhile. . . . Bobbing hair is one of those things that show us whether we are abreast of the age in which we find ourselves."

By then many middle-aged and older women had followed their "dancing daughters" to the barber's chair, and among younger women bobbed hair was almost universal. Whether to bob or not was no longer a stormy question. With the help of permanent waving the severely boyish look was replaced with longer bobs, with windblown effects, and with cheek-caressing spit curls that some critics called "hardly respectable." High fashion tried to ignore the extremes of Hollywood, but for the young it was the film stars who set the style.

Clara Bow was the girl who had "It," the potent sex appeal and bold personality that typified the Flapper and the New Girl of the Jazz Age. As the celluloid symbol of the girl who smoked, drank, and danced until dawn in revolt against the hypocrisy of old-fashioned morality, she was envied by thousands who wanted to show the world they were part of "It," at least to the extent of imitating her cheek curls and the short-cropped fringe of her forehead bangs.

Young male "sheiks" of the early 1920s adopted the long sideburns and slicked-back pompadour they hoped would give their hair the "patent leather" look of Rudolph Valentino's. Others went to the opposite direction and waved their hair, some borrowing technique from their girl friends to have it Marcelled. But by 1930 the "patent leather" look was out for men, along with hair parted at the center, and women's hair had started a new upward trend. It was temporarily halted in mid-climb by another shockwave from Hollywood.

The moment in 1941 was recorded exactly by *Life* magazine. "The 49th minute of the movie *I Wanted Wings,*" it reported, was "marked as one of the historic moments of the cinema . . . when an unknown young actress named Veronica Lake walked into camera range and waggled a head of long blonde hair at a suddenly enchanted public."

Falling across the side of her face, covering one eye and sometimes both, it tumbled to eight inches below her shoulders, sheep-dog

124

style. Most men, who hadn't seen such long hair since bobbing began, acclaimed it. Some writers dubbed it the "strip-tease hair-do," claiming it provoked male visions of a modern Lady Godiva. Moralists, who not long before had been thundering against the "wickedness" of bobbed hair, viewed the new style with alarm. Bobbed haired mothers chorused their disapproval, but their daughters by the hundreds copied Veronica Lake's long hair. For some, the copies were made of pinned-on false hair.

Within months, the fad died, smothered by newer Hollywood images of the long bob. By the time America entered the Second World War, even long bobbed hair had become impractical for most women. Many

Veronica Lake.   *United Press International, Inc.*

who ran the factories of war production, where free-flowing locks might be caught in machinery, just bagged up the curls at the backs of their heads into net snoods, in a practical revival of 17th century fashion.

Hair went to the tops of women's heads in 1945 in topknots that some critics said made their wearers look like "yesteryear's washerwoman." Brushed up from the roots to a mass of curls at the top, the hair was tied close to the head with a string, and then the part above the string was combed down or pinned under to form topknot circlets and crowns called "sausages" and "doughnuts." The "rats" that had been worn at the start of the century came back as hair cushions used to pad out the new head-top rolls.

The topknots fell down into pony tails as teen-age girls of the early 1950s began wearing their hair straight, combed toward the crown and gathered into a single loose tail of hair secured with a rubber band near the scalp. Barbarian tribesmen in Europe had worn it much the same way back in the year 50 B.C.

Soon there was a new hair battle raging. The dilemma confronting "thousands of American women," according to *Life* magazine, was whether they wanted to "look like horses or poodles." Challenging the pony tail and the somewhat sleeker and longer horse tail was the new tousled short-haired poodle clip, which required 125 curlers to produce its Medusa-like confusion, and needed cutting every two weeks, as well as frequent permanents for those whose hair was naturally straight.

While most teen-agers kept their ponys, smart hairdressing salons reported poodling hundreds of heads a day. Among the poodle-dos were such movie and television stars as Peggy Ann Garner, Ann Sothern, and Faye Emerson, but many women hesitated for fear the poodle clip would be another quickly passing fad that would leave them shorn and sorry. Hairdressers were all for it, since it meant more income. When a columnist wrote, "Poodle haircuts are strictly for dogs," one hairdresser answered, "Everybody knows where horses' tails belong."

Italian movies shown in the United States started still another vogue to complicate the situation, with the short, shaggy Italian cut that required as much constant clipping as the poodle. Sculptured in "messy waves" on the crown, with spit curls framing forehead and cheeks, it was carefully ragged at the nape of the neck. As a romantic women's magazine editor explained, "It's like your boyfriend has been nibbling at the back of your neck."

Men meanwhile were going through a hair revolution of their own. Those who entered the armed forces in the early 1940s had military haircuts forced upon them. The Army's G.I. cut clipped hair to a maximum length of one and one-half inches and Navy cuts were as short. Accepted with much grumbling, they and the combat styles of the military years to come inspired hero worshipers to imitate them. Civilian males took to the crew cut, the even shorter butch, and the precision-cut flattop. Bristly short hair, sometimes stiffened upright with wax, became the dominant male style for some twenty years.

Modern crew cut. A far cry from the cropped crew cuts of the 1950s was the stylized version that survived another twenty years, such as this one created in 1970 by New Britain, Conn., barber Dominic Gulli (Local 316). *Barbers, Beauticians and Allied Industries International Ass'n., AFL-CIO-CLC*

The flattop, which applied a geometrical trim to the common crew cut, was being demanded by forty per cent of barbershop customers in 1956. Crew cuts by then had changed the popular image of the American hero. Girls of the early 1950s were getting goose-pimples over "common garden males . . . who squint through horned-rimmed glasses and whose crew cuts look as if the owner's head had just been browsed by an undecided sheep," *Life* reported in 1951, citing as examples television's Dave Garroway and musical comedy star Russell Nype. A whole new crop of young actors had "sprouted with the coltish, wet-behind-the-ears look of high school sophomores." Actresses were offering feminine versions, such as those worn by Mary Martin in *South Pacific* and Carol Channing in a musical revival of the 1920s *Gentlemen Prefer Blondes.*

When high school and college girls also began to imitate the male crew cut, columnist Robert Ruark wrote that it was getting so "you have to ask for a draft card to tell boys from girls." The "nadir of the short haircut" was the feminine butch, described by one critic as "an attempt by girls to look more male than men." Some couples displayed matching His and Hers butch cuts. "The name 'butch' comes from 'butcher,' " one writer pointed out, "and the girls look like their hair came from his hamburger machine."

Some men, in revolt against the crew cut, shaved all the hair off their heads to go bald like film star Yul Brynner, and some let it grow long enough to have it fan waved with comb and dryer by such barbers as were beginning to call themselves "men's hairstylists." But for most men, the crew cut endured.

The first great threat to the crew cut came from Elvis Presley. Men's hair was short, music was mostly sweet and sentimental, and teen-agers were still a sub-culture in an adult world when Presley burst upon the scene in 1956. His pouting look, hip-grinding sexuality, and the sharp, explosive sound of his rocking music that mixed crooning with the hard beat of black rhythm and blues in a new blend that sold millions of records, gave teen-agers an idol set apart from adults. Parents, teachers, preachers, and culture critics denounced him, but to many of the young he became a hero and a leader.

Challenging the bristly crew cut, his combed-back blue-black hair, with "a lank hank over the forehead and a grippable tuft in front of each ear," became a symbol of new teen independence. Even girls

Elvis Presley. *RCA Records.*

OPPOSITE PAGE "We must learn to adapt to changing fashions," said Chief of Naval Operations, Admiral Zumwalt, as he announced in 1970 that no Navy officers or enlisted men were to be "in any way penalized during the time they are growing beards, moustaches or sideburns." *Official U.S. Navy photograph.*

128

wanted hair like Presley's. Not satisfied just to adore him, they swarmed into barbershops to surrender their pony tails and have their hair clipped Presley-style. One seventeen-year-old Michigan girl carried her pony tail home in a paper bag and announced, "Look, ma, no hair." Others gave their shorn locks as souvenirs to brothers and boyfriends. Some boyfriends as well as protesting fathers were outraged.

Then in 1958 Presley was drafted. Uncle Sam cut off his hair and side-burns and he became a model soldier, his hair clipped to Middle American and his music softened for a time to sentimental ballads. On most male heads, the crew cut survived into the 1960s, but Presley had helped shape what was to come, in music and in hair. Looking back, the *London Times* would say that "from him a whole generation took its life style." It was from England that rock music and long hair would come sweeping back across the United States.

Women's hair in the late 1950s and early 1960s started back toward the 18th century. Thick pageboy hair-dos were teased and crossed with clouds of lacquer from push-button cans of hair spray to produce mushroom mops that bulged to a width of fourteen inches at the sides. Then they bubbled into beehives and artichokes and began an upward thrust that was helped by the popularity of Jacqueline Kennedy's brioche, a long loose bob with a large bun on the crown, in hairy replica of the sweet roll Parisians eat for breakfast.

Soon "cotton candy bouffants," filched from the age of Louis XIV, were towering atop women's heads, to the annoyance of Broadway theatergoers who filled newspapers with letters of complaint about having to sit behind them. School officials in Chicago, where eighty per cent of teen-age girls took to wearing them, and in Detroit, Los Angeles, and elsewhere, also complained that bouffants were blocking the classroom view of teacher, distracting school work, causing collisions between hair and doorways. As in the 18th century there was criticism that some towering headpieces were unsanitary because the lacquered set-pieces were worn too long between shampoos.

"Among teen-agers," *Newsweek* reported in March, 1962, "bouffants are proliferating as fast as the toadstools they resemble." For those ignorant of the engineering involved, the magazine explained: "Hold the hair straight out, tease it with a comb until it gets frizzled, then comb some of the outside hair over this big mess of frizzled-up hair and set it in place with a cloud of hair spray."

Fashionable women, who had it done by hairdressers, found themselves engaged in a torture of comb-wielding that stood their hair on end all over their heads before it was raked into shape for the spraying, which often required covering the nose and face with a protective mask, as 18th century ladies had during hair powdering. But they were so pleased by the results, they courted the attention of hairdressers who became international celebrities because of their patronage.

Again, it was the age of the hairdresser, in which some stylists achieved the status held long before by the coiffeurs of royalty. Even among hairdressers, however, there were those who predicted that the artificial hair-teasing craze would not last long. "Men hate it," one Hollywood beauty expert said. "They want to see a woman's hair bobble freely as she walks."

And then . . . came the 1964 invasion of the Beatles to trigger the American war over hair that raged through the decade. By 1970, youth had made its hair protest and had toppled the barricades. Its victory had carried well into the ranks of the once short-haired over-30 gen-

130

From the musical "Hair"

131

eration, and longer hair was tolerated almost everywhere, at least in moderation if not always at hippie-length.

Early classroom skirmishes over hair had faded into the past along with "Beatlemania" by the time delegates of the 200,000-member American Federation of Teachers voted in national convention at Pittsburgh in August, 1970, to support student "freedom of speech and expression, including a choice of one's own dress and grooming." True, a national public opinion poll that year showed that fifty-four per cent of a cross-section of Americans still were against "new styles in hair." But the lingering opposition was hardly reflected in the view from the streets, where longer hair, as well as sideburns, moustaches, and beards, had achieved eminent respectability.

Doctors, lawyers, corporation executives, poets, athletes, the butcher, baker, and almost any candlestick-maker, paraded hair proudly, side by side with youth. Respectable long hair had become gray with middle age, ubiquitous from coast to coast. Youth, with an assist from the world of fashion, the arts, advertising, and popular singers, actors, and brawny football stars, had brought about the start of an era of "anything goes" in hair style.

Long hair, in fact, had become so much a part of the establishment there were predictions of a new revolt that would turn the historic cycle back to short hair again. Barbers should keep their sense of perspective, president Joseph DePaola of the Barbers, Beauticians and Allied Industries union told them, and remember "hair-length fashion has always changed and always will."

In London, where the long hair trend first started, there already were skinheads, bands of slum area boys who roamed the streets in gangs to terrorize anybody who aroused their savage prejudice, particularly Pakistani immigrants and "hairies," the long-haired young they hated. They shunned girls, modern music, soccer games, and were the self-appointed puritanical foes of all that was swinging London and middle class "flash." One million strong, the largest teen group since the days of the rockers, the skinheads shaved their hair to within an eighth of an inch of their scalps. Wanting none of their savagery, but borrowing their short-cropped hair style, a leading Mayfair hairdresser provided skinhead hair-dos for some of London's trendiest ladies. There were those who wondered if the skinned heads were the first temblor of a new teen hairquake that would shake America.

Avant-garde fashion designers saw the coming not only of short hair, but of heads and faces shaved of all hair, with both men and women completely bald. They predicted that, like the ancient Egyptians, every-

132

body would do away with the nuisance of natural hair and wear wigs, stylized as Egyptian wigs once were, not to resemble hair at all but to serve as synthetic head coverings designed for winter warmth or summer comfort.

Eventually today's longhairs will be the older generation, perhaps the ones to rise in fury against a new short-haired generation. But perhaps the revolt of the 1960s had achieved a greater victory than the right to wear hair long, a tolerance for the appearance of others, whether their hair was long, short or absent entirely, the dawning of an age when one human no longer snap-judged another by his color, accent, dress, or haircut. That could be what it was really all about. It *could* be.

☛ *Index* ☚

134